SOUTHWARK
ILLUSTRATED HISTORY

BY LEONARD REILLY

London Borough of Southwark

Acknowledgments

This book is the fruit of many people's labour. My first and deepest thanks must go to colleagues and predecessors at Southwark Local Studies Library. Stephen Humphrey (archivist) and Stephen Potter have read and commented on the text in its various drafts and saved me from numerous unnecessary errors, suggested improvements, directed me towards sources for illustrations and helped with details too small to mention. Other colleagues, Maggie de Bristowe, Duncan Bonner, Anna Dolling and Denise King have also kept the library operating during the increasingly frantic later stages of preparation. I must thank Dominic Bean, Southwark Libraries' Marketing Officer, for seeing the project through its early dangerous journey from inception to approval and funding.

Equally gratitude is due to those who have preceded me as Southwark's Local Studies Librarian; Janice Brooker, Nicola Smith, Bernard Nurse and Mary Boast. They have ensured that the collection and its organisation is one of the finest in London. Mary Boast deserves particular mention as she amalgamated the local collections of the three Metropolitan Boroughs and started the publication by the Council of local history books with the production of the series of neighbourhood histories. In spirit, and to some degree content, this book is a colourful culmination of these.

I thank my wife Sarah, who not only listened for many hours to innumerable details about the book's production, but also much more importantly took the rigorous pen of the professional editor to a less than polished text and helped it to shine. The book was designed and seen through print by Carol Enright, who, as she has done many times, brings visual flair and an almost unnatural calmness to a fraught process. It was printed by Battley Brothers Ltd. of Clapham.

I claim acknowledgement for the mistakes.

The following individuals and institutions are gratefully thanked for giving permission to reproduce their images: Inside cover and p.14 (top) the Trustees of the Chatsworth Settlement; facing p.1 (right) Cities Revealed, Geointernational, ©Financial Times Professional Ltd 1998; p.3 (left) Museum of London Archaeology Service; p.4 Museum of London Picture Library; p.6 Museum of London Archaeology Service; p.17 Peter Froste; p.9 The Iveagh Bequest/English Heritage Photo Library; p.17 (top) Museum of London Picture Library; p.18 (bottom) The Marquees of Salisbury; p.23, p.25 (bottom) Guildhall Library Corporation of London/Bridgman Art Library; p.34 ©The National Gallery; p.35 and p.38 (top) Lambeth Archives; p.5 (top and bottom) Museum in Docklands Project PLA Collection; p.69 (right) Aerofilms Ltd.; p.71 London Metropolitan Archives; p.78 (bottom left) Sport & General Picture Agency; p.83 and 85 (top right) L B Southwark Press Office; p.86 Sunday Telegraph; p.88 L B Southwark Press Office; p.89 (top left) Roy White, Jubilee Line Extension; p.89 (bottom Left) Graham Cook, Jubilee Line Extension. All other images are part of the collection at Southwark Local Studies Library.

Published 1998. © London Borough of Southwark

Southwark Local Studies Library, 211 Borough High Street, London SE1 IJA

ISBN 0 905849 23 X

British Library Cataloguing in Publication data. A catalogue record for this book is available from the British Library.

Southwark Council

Contents

CHAPTER 1

Introduction

Southwark has one of the widest ranges of historical experience and landscape in London. Its history is as distinguished as that of its neighbours, the City and Westminster. Its contribution to the London and national scene, though markedly different from theirs, is of equal importance. It claims with justification the title of London's most historic borough.

The present Borough of Southwark has a river frontage of four and a half miles opposite the City of London, the Tower and Limehouse. It stretches south for just over five miles to Dulwich and Crystal Palace to form a roughly symmetrical triangle.

The Borough was formed in 1965 from the Metropolitan Boroughs of Southwark, Bermondsey and Camberwell. These in turn were amalgamations of the ancient civil parishes of Christ Church, Blackfriars Road; Saint Saviour; Saint Thomas; Saint Olave; Saint George the Martyr; Saint Mary, Newington; Saint John, Horselydown; Saint Mary Magdalen, Bermondsey; Saint Mary, Rotherhithe

and Saint Giles, Camberwell. Until the formation of the London County Council in 1889 it was part of the County of Surrey.

The core of the town of Southwark, confusingly also called The Borough, has been at the heart of London's history for 2000 years. Its particular contributions have been in the fields of transport, industry and entertainment. The other ancient communities of Bermondsey and Rotherhithe also have distinctive characteristics. The former has been noted for industry, particularly tanning and food processing, and the latter for its river-related activities of ship building and repair and for its docks. In the 19th century, parts of Bermondsey were among the most overcrowded and insanitary in the whole of Britain. As with other parts of north Southwark, they have undergone tremendous redevelopment over the centuries and only tantalising glimpses of their original townscapes remain.

Rather more survives of Southwark's inner suburbs, Newington, Walworth and north Camberwell. Essentially rural until the late 18th and early 19th

centuries, these areas were developed largely as a result of the building of new bridges over the Thames.

Farther south, Peckham, East Dulwich, Camberwell and Nunhead were developed in the late 19th century as suburbs of uniform respectable working class housing linked to the metropolis by railways and trams.

Dulwich's development is apart from this general pattern. At its centre is Dulwich College and its associated estate. Development here has been carefully controlled by the College and the area retains an affluent and in places rural character, quite different to the intensely urban and post-industrial townscape only a few miles north.

The sources available to help us learn about this past are almost as varied as the past itself. In addition to a distinguished list of published books - many antiquarian and others current and academic - there are a huge number of primary sources available. These sources mainly relate to later periods. Our knowledge of Southwark's very early history, however, is almost entirely due to the

Top:
Affluent, suburban Dulwich: middle England.

Bottom:
The inner-city: Walworth.

work of archaeologists. Despite its proximity to London, where there has been a long tradition of archaeology, it was only relatively recently that many of the most exciting archaeological finds were made. These have radically altered our view of Southwark's early history. Ironically, one of the factors facilitating this expansion of our knowledge has been the amount of recent redevelopment in the borough. It is now incumbent on developers to give archaeologists the time and funds to allow for excavations prior to redevelopment. As a result many areas have been investigated only recently for the first time. Despite this our knowledge is still partial, limited by the time available for excavations, the boundaries of the site being developed and sometimes by ground disturbance of more recent years.

Documentary sources start in quantity for the 16th and 17th centuries and expand greatly in the 18th and particularly the 19th. They are principally the records of local government; the Vestries and Metropolitan Boroughs at local level and the Metropolitan Board of

Works, the London County Council and later the Greater London Council at the Metropolitan level. Many of the most interesting sources are not text based. Among visual sources, Southwark has been recorded on many of London's panoramas providing a lively and detailed foreground to views of the City. Southwark has also been comprehensively illustrated by artists from Hogarth and Turner to more minor but prolific ones such as Edward Yates or, in the modern period, David Hepher, who has been inspired by brutal post-war tower blocks or Tom Phillips, who has photographed the same twenty scenes in Peckham on the same day each year since 1973. Fortunately most map-makers have not heeded the niceties of administrative boundaries and consequently Southwark is shown in many of the most important maps of London. More well known, but perhaps less helpful as an objective historical source, has been Southwark's place in literature. Chaucer and Shakespeare, though having links to the town, tell us little, but Dickens vividly recreated the townscape, people and atmosphere of the Victorian period. He speaks more eloquently than any dry report. The area's role as a muse continues to the present day: it is the a setting for much rose-tinted popular historical fiction and, by contrast, for *Last Orders*, Graham Swift's gritty view of a bizarre Bermondsey funeral. Peckham is home to one of the BBC's most popular and enduring comic creations: Del and Rodney of Trotter's Independent Trading Company.

Left:
An archaeological excavation under Borough High Street during work building the ticket hall to the new London Bridge Station, part of the Jubilee Line Extension, 1995.

Above:
Charles Dickens.

CHAPTER 2

Early history

To understand when, how and why the area was first inhabited and subsequently changed, it is essential to gain a picture of Southwark's landscape stripped of its man-made features. Southwark's natural features have played a determining role in its pattern of settlement for the whole of its history and until relatively recent times.

In pre-Roman and Roman times the natural landscape of what is Southwark was radically different to that of today. This landscape was dominated by the River Thames. The Thames was then much wider - up to half a mile across - and much lower. At the time of the Roman occupation it was tidal probably to no farther than London itself. Most of the area, up to a mile or more inland from the river's edge, was part of a huge, fertile but undrained flood plain.

This huge, marshy area was broken by a number of small gravel islands. There were three roughly along the line of Borough High Street, another farther east in Horselydown and another in Bermondsey. A causeway ran south to another at the present Elephant & Castle and there was another at St George's Circus. These islands were crucial in the development of Roman Southwark and by extension Roman London.

Southwark's first permanent residents considerably predate the Romans, the very earliest dating from 8,000 years ago, barely after the last ice-age had receded. Our evidence is a find of a large number of worked flints, many still very sharp, discovered just north of the Old Kent Road. More significant was the discovery at a site in Wolseley Street in Bermondsey of plough marks in the soil thought to date from 1,500 BC. Marks of this sort are very rare and show two important things: that there were permanent occupants living by agriculture and also that the river, at that time, did not flood the area. The site survived because the Thames rose in the post-Roman period flooding the area and so preventing development and disturbance.

Roman Southwark, which it must be called as there is no known Roman name, originated as the southern approach to the crossing of the River Thames. It is more accurate to say that London owes its position to Southwark as it was the succession of low gravel islands amid the marsh on the river's south side that allowed an approach road to a crossing place to be built. There is evidence of a major fire in about AD 60. This may have been an accident or may have been part of Boudica, the Queen of the Britons', sacking of the City. If the latter were the case, and evidence is only circumstantial, it would further establish Southwark's position as an important early settlement.

The bridge was built sometime between AD 50 and 70, some years after the first occupation. Its site was about 60 yards downstream of the present London Bridge. New houses made of stone were built along the approach road but farther from the road's edge so allowing more space for vehicles and pedestrians. The road had a gravel surface and an arcade or colonnade at its side, and the town may have had a market. The settlement incorporated high quality buildings some with mosaic floors and under-floor heating. Their

Left:
An artists impression of Southwark's iron age landscape.

5

functions are uncertain but suggested uses have been residential and military. There was a baths on the site of the present London Bridge Station. It was at this time that Roman Southwark reached its greatest extent; it may have covered up to 45 acres and been about 15% the size of the City. As with London, whose fortunes it mirrored, it contracted in the 3rd century before the final abandonment of the colony by the Romans in AD 410.

In addition to Borough High Street, its southerly continuation, Kennington Park Road, and the Old Kent Road are of Roman origin. Stane Street, which is the precursor of Newington Causeway and Kennington Park Road, had its junction with Watling Street, the precursor of the Old Kent Road, on one of the low gravel island at the present junction of Borough High Street and Tabard Street. Stane Street's final destination was Chichester and Watling Street's Dover. There is also sketchier evidence of two other Roman roads. One, it is claimed, went to Lewes diverging from the Old Kent Road and following the present Asylum Road. It is claimed that another, for which there is even less evidence, ran south west from London Bridge towards a ferry crossing of the river at Lambeth.

Information on Southwark (or indeed London) is scarce for the period after the Romans abandoned Britain. It is likely that the City and Southwark were abandoned, possibly for 450 years. It is almost certain too that the bridge disappeared.

In this period significant changes took place to the natural landscape of the area. The River Thames rose, and became more vigorously tidal, flooding a much wider area and limiting the possibility of recolonisation.

Below:
A Roman oil lamp in the shape of a right foot found under Borough High Street during the Jubilee Line excavations.

Opposite:
An aerial view of Roman London in c.AD 75 by Peter Froste.

CHAPTER 3
The Medieval and Pre-Reformation period: 1100-1540

Above:
The parish church of St Saviour in c. 1750.

Opposite:
London Bridge in 1639, a painting by C de Jongh

Southwark is not heard of again until c.910, during a period of great turbulence in English history. The name *Suthringa geworche*, the defensive work of the men of Surrey, is the first appearance of its modern name. This name was later corrupted to mean the southern defences (to the City). It is likely that Southwark was at that time little more than a garrison station defending the recently rebuilt bridge from Viking invaders. Two events, both of which may have expanded in the telling, show the vulnerability of London to Norse attack. The first is the account of how the Norwegian king Olav destroyed London Bridge by attaching his ships to it and rowing vigorously, assisted by the tide. The second concerns the Danish king Cnut who, prevented by the bridge from access to London from the south or east, dug a ditch through the marsh south of Southwark, dragged his ships through it and was able to besiege London from the west.

In the more peaceable succeeding century the settlement grew largely in response to London's expansion. Southwark is described in Domesday Book, where a Minster church, probably the same institution that developed into the Priory of St Mary Overie, and a dock, are mentioned.

In the 13th and 14th centuries the town centred around the approach to London Bridge which was rebuilt in stone by 1209. This bridge remained the only river crossing near London until 1750. The town extended south down the high street (sometimes this was called Long Southwark), west along Bankside and east along Tooley Street. Later, ribbon development took place along Kent Street (the present Tabard Street and main road to Kent), farther south on the high street beyond this junction along the high street and along Bermondsey Street.

The town's principal buildings were the Priory of St Mary Overie, its five parish churches, the hospital of St Thomas and the palaces and houses of the wealthy citizens. These houses were often associated with the important prelates of the day. The Bishop of Winchester's palace is the most famous, but others included those of the Abbot of Battle, and the Prior of Lewes.

Borough High Street was lined on both sides by numerous inns. Due to the narrowness of London Bridge and a lack of accommodation in the City, Southwark was the terminus for travellers to London from south of the Thames. The inns served as the arrival and departure point for travellers and provided short and long term accommodation for visitors to London. This temporary population brought a lively and cosmopolitan character to the town. Chaucer's pilgrims started from a real Inn, the Tabard, (later Talbot), having been looked after by a real host, Harry Bailey.

Bankside, which stretched half a mile west along the river front, had a rather different character. It was lined with brothels or stews. The City had made an effective job of expelling the brothels but Southwark, with its easy, access from and to London and weaker administration, was an ideal location. The Bishop of Winchester, in whose manor the brothels were, made spirited but largely unsuccessful attempts to regulate their activities.

Above:
Borough High Street sometimes called Long Southwark, looking north. From the panorama of London by Wyngaerde. The perspective has been greatly distorted to make the High Street appear shorter than it is. There are also inaccuracies: the church with the tower in the right foreground is St George the Martyr but it should be at the road junction in the immediate foreground. The ornate building on the left foreground is Suffolk Place, the palace of Charles Brandon.

Inland from Bankside, at its eastern end, was the Bishop of Winchester's park. In the later medieval period much of the area immediately inland from Bankside was given over to commercial fishponds. Farther inland again was the poorly drained, semi-marsh of St George's fields, which acted as the town's common.

The town was administered through five manors; Paris Garden, the Clink, the King's, the Guildable and the Great Liberty. Their total area coincided with the later civil parishes of Christ Church, St George the Martyr, St Thomas, St Olave, and St John, Horselydown. Some of the manors exercised a high degree of autonomy, largely exempt from, Crown, Church and the City. Paris Garden, for example, which was at the town's western extremity, offered sanctuary to felons. The City

saw Southwark as both a nuisance and a potential source of revenue and a threat and, from the 14th century onwards, attempted to gain administrative control. In the face of resistance, the City was partly successful and managed to accrue limited powers over taxation and the arrest of felons. The town on the other hand also took steps to assert its independence. From 1295 onwards it was allowed to send two representatives to parliament but, despite later adopting the name The Borough, it never achieved the formal status of a borough, confirmed by a charter and headed by a mayor.

Southwark has been characterised as the repository for the undesirable, but entirely natural elements that any urban area generates. In addition to the prostitutes and to criminals seeking sanctuary there were others.

Above:
A romanticised 18th century view of the departure of Chaucer's pilgrims leaving the Tabard Inn.

Left:
The Bishop of Winchester's Palace in 1640. The surviving rose window formed the gable end of the main hall to the rear of the buildings. In the middle ages the Clink prison was in the rooms that surrounded the inner wooded courtyard in the foreground. St Mary Overie's dock is on the extreme right.

The town was home to up to five prisons. The Marshalsea and the King's Bench were royal prisons. Later additions were the Counter, a further crown institution and the White Lion, the Surrey County prison. The Bishop of Winchester also had his own, the Clink, for those found guilty by the manorial court. All these prisons were characterised by appalling conditions and corrupt administration.

Economically Southwark provided much employment in the high street inns but the town was also the home to polluting or dangerous trades and to those who wished to trade exempt from the City's regulations. Examples of such trades are leather working, brewing and military supply. A number of those who worked in these areas were aliens or immigrants. The town had London's largest immigrant

population, mainly Dutch or German people excluded by the City ostensibly because they were not members of one of the trade guilds. Fishing and the operation of tidemills were also important to the economy of the riverside communities. The river was much cleaner than at present and remained so for many years: a salmon was reported at Rotherhithe in 1800.

In 1460 the Crown granted to the City permission to hold a fair in Southwark. From its earliest days it was a boisterous affair lasting two weeks and sited at the southern end of Borough High Street.

Bermondsey and Rotherhithe

A mile or so to the east of Southwark was the settlement of Bermondsey. Its principal feature was a major monastic house, Bermondsey Priory (later Abbey). This was founded in 1082 and the first monks, from the Cluniac order, arrived when the buildings were completed seven years later. It occupied a site on the low gravel island surrounded by marsh. The meaning of the *ey* element in Bermondsey's name refers to this island. In later years the Abbey benefited from various

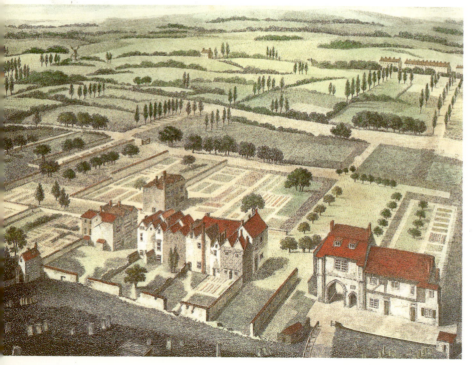

Left:
Bermondsey Abbey. The remains as recorded by C J M Whichelo in 1805. The view is looking south. St Mary Magdalen's churchyard is in the foreground and the gatehouse is in the right foreground.

endowments of land, often from the Crown. Its functions were more than just spiritual. It was an important centre of learning, and, in its position as lord of the manor of Bermondsey and Rotherhithe, it was responsible for the draining of the marsh and maintenance of a river wall. The Abbey was dissolved by Henry VIII in 1538. Almost nothing remains of the fabric of the monastery, but Bermondsey Square is the site of the inner courtyard and Grange Road follows the line of the road leading to the monastery's farm or grange. The church of St Mary Magdalen originated as the church for the Abbey's lay workers.

The leather industry, for which Bermondsey was to become famous, was first referred to in the late 14th century. The required raw materials were readily available: skins came from the City butchers, water from local streams, notably the Neckinger, and oak bark from nearby woodland. Skilled craftsmen to work the tanned leather were well represented in the area's immigrant community.

Other settlements were more modest in scale. For some, their place name is among the most interesting and fullest evidence as to their character.

Rotherhithe probably means a place where cattle were landed and so alludes to the maritime links that characterised it in later years. Rotherhithe is effectively a peninsula and Rotherhithe Street, which started life as the river wall, follows the wide bend in the Thames. Much of the parish was low lying and remained for many centuries a patchwork of marsh and pasture intersected by drainage ditches. It was in one sense an inside-out parish, as until the docks were built in the early 19th century, its principal features were nearer its boundary than its centre. Rotherhithe became a separate manor in the 12th century. Aside from the parish church of St Mary the Virgin its most significant medieval building was the royal manor house built by Edward III on the riverfront at Platform Wharf at the west end of the parish.

Much of the land farther south, Newington, Walworth and St George's fields, was undrained marsh. This was interrupted by three areas of higher ground. Two of these were gravel islands, one at the junction of Newington Street, later Butts and Walworth Road, and one at the site of the later St George's Circus. The third was a ridge of land, later called a causeway, carrying the road to Southwark. This area contained two settlements. Newington, the 'new town' was settled on the higher, drained ground near the road junction. It was first heard of in the 13th century. The older and larger Walworth, its name means 'the farm of the Britons', was along the track leading south. Farther south again was Camberwell.

By the time of the Domesday Book, Camberwell was important enough to have its own church. The origin of the first part of Camberwell's name is uncertain, it may mean crooked or sick or it may be a reference to Cymru, the Welsh. The origin of the second part is obvious, indeed there were wells in Camberwell Grove until the early years of this century. Camberwell was a very large parish and included the hamlets of Peckham and Dulwich. The manor of Dulwich was part of Bermondsey Abbey's lands.

CHAPTER 4

The Early Modern Period: 1530-1700

The period from the 1530s to 1700 saw a dramatic increase in London's size both from what it had been up to that time, and proportionally in relation to other English towns. This had important effects on Southwark which became closer to the City of London in character and administration and also on the areas of Bermondsey and Rotherhithe.

Southwark

In the town of Southwark many of the characteristics of the medieval town continued; the inns, the prisons, the industries, the aliens and the prostitutes. As a result of immigration the population grew from around 10,000 in 1547 to double that by 1600 and 30,000 by 1678. The population did not grow evenly, as the predations of various diseases halted its growth. The area was hit especially badly in 1625 and 1634.

Southwark's population represented more than 10% of London's population and in the 17th century it was the second largest urban area in England. The population would have included a highly transitory group using the inns and a reluctant permanent one in the prisons.

Expansion took place initially along the riverfront west to Paris Garden Stairs (just east of the present Blackfriars Bridge) and east, infilling the area between Tooley Street and the river. There was also ribbon development along Blackman Street (that part of the present Borough High Street south of St George's church) and along Bermondsey Street. Later building took place south of Tooley Street, along Kent Street (now Tabard Street), along Long Lane and west on Bankside to the Old Barge House (the present borough boundary near the Oxo tower). Less building than one might expect took

place on the still extensive open space south of Bankside as these areas, the Bishop of Winchester's park and the manor of Paris Garden, were below the high water level, badly drained and susceptible to flooding. This situation changed little with the sale of the manor of Paris Garden in 1660 and the creation of a new parish of Christ Church in 1671. This did not herald immediate development as the fate of the new parish church, which had to be pulled down after 50 years due to subsidence, gave a warning to builders and potential residents alike. By 1700 there were only a few tentative streets in the area.

Southwark was dramatically altered by two extensive fires, one in 1676 in the northern part of the town and the other in 1689 in the south. Together they necessitated the rebuilding of almost all the buildings along the high street including the inns.

The character of Bankside also changed with the development of other forms of entertainment. Bear-baiting and the theatres, which the City saw as equally disreputable and did not wish to host, became established. The bear ring was visited by the establishment of the day and was often written of approvingly. Edward Alleyn, actor and founder of Dulwich College, was appointed Master of the Royal Bears in 1604. The last bear pit closed in 1682, long outliving the theatres.

There were four Bankside theatres, the Rose, the Swan, the Hope (which at times doubled as a bear ring) and the Globe. The Globe, which opened in 1599, though not the largest, has become the most famous as it belonged to the group of actors called the King's men of which William Shakespeare was a member. It was rebuilt in 1613 after a serious fire. All leading playwrights of the day including Christopher Marlowe and Ben Johnson and actors including Richard Burbage spent much of their careers on Bankside. The Rose and the Swan closed in the early years of the 17th century and the Globe

and the Hope were closed after the performing of plays was prohibited in 1642.

The middle years of the 16th century were ones of great upheaval nationally and locally. The changes brought by the Reformation did not leave Southwark untouched. The priory church of St Mary was closed and the building became the church for the new parish of St Saviour, an amalgamation of the earlier parishes of St Mary Magdalen and St Margaret. Southwark also became a centre for the more ardent forms of Protestantism, partly due to the numbers of continental immigrants in the area and partly due to religious dissenters in local prisons. A number of Southwark people were among the pioneer settlers in New England, their departure in part prompted by a wish to exercise freely their Protestant beliefs

Another famous emigrant to the colonies was John Harvard. He was the son of a wealthy Southwark butcher and inn-keeper and settled in Charlestown, near Boston in 1637. At his death he left land and his library

towards the foundation of a college and it is in this bequest that Harvard University has its origin.

This period also saw a rapid and important change in land holding and the alteration of the administrative relationship between Southwark and the City. In an attempt to establish a new palace Henry VIII acquired much land in Southwark. His plan collapsed, but, for the first time in its history, much of Southwark was now administered by one body, the Crown. This gave the City, which had long been frustrated by what it saw as its neighbour's threatening autonomy, an opportunity to add to the rights it had been acquiring over Southwark during previous centuries. This it did in 1550 when it bought from the Crown, for £980, three manors; the Guildable, the Great Liberty and the Kings. This part of the town was incorporated into the City as Bridge Ward Without and technically remained part of the City until 1900. Unfortunately for the City the rights that allowed these manors the independence the City disapproved of were not withdrawn, the other town's other manors (Clink and Paris

Right
Cure's College
Almshouses.
A watercolour of c. 1852
by Thomas Shepherd.

Below:
The Southwark theatres
shown in Hollar's
panorama of 1636-42.

Garden) were not purchased,
so Southwark's independence was
substantially unaltered.

The Duke of Suffolk, Charles
Brandon, built a palace on the high
street on land sold to him by Henry
VIII. Briefly it housed a royal mint.
The palace features prominently in
Tudor views of Southwark.

Services started to develop. The
parishes of St Saviour in 1562 and
St Olave in 1571 established grammar
schools. Cure's College, an almshouse,
was founded in 1584 on Park Street.

Bermondsey and Rotherhithe

At the dissolution Bermondsey Abbey
was eventually acquired by Thomas
Pope and with its stone the mansion
of Bermondsey House was erected in
c.1550. It later became the Earl of
Sussex's town house. Thomas Pope
founded Trinity College Oxford and
it is possible some of Bermondsey's
books ended up in the college library.
The parish's fortunes rose at the end
of the 17th century as demonstrated
by the rebuilding of St Mary's church
in 1680. A new parish of St John

Above:
The Howland Great Wet Dock in
1717. Note its remote situation,
the trees surrounding it (to
provide shelter from storms) the
small size of boats using it, and
the other wet and dry docks
along the riverside.

Opposite:
A wedding at Horselydown
c. 1566. It is probably the
wedding of the daughter of the
Earl of Sussex.

Horselydown was founded in 1733, the cost of the new building coming, like many other of London churches of that date, from the proceeds of a tax on coal.

The riverfront became important as overseas and domestic trade expanded. Landing places near the City were at a premium and the warehouses of the Upper Pool (the reach just downstream from London Bridge) were built. The Hay's Wharf Company, which was to become one of the larger wharfingers, was founded in 1651. Bermondsey also became a centre for entertainment. The Jamaica House on the road to Deptford was a popular tavern, and there was a pleasure garden visited by Samuel Pepys at Cherry Garden.

Rotherhithe gained from Britain's overseas expansion. Its services in ship building, repairing and breaking were required by the Royal Navy and the East India Company. Both extensively used the Naval dockyard just downstream at Deptford but at times of peak demand, particularly when the country was at war, much work came to Rotherhithe. More

significantly Rotherhithe was the site chosen for the building of only the second wet dock in London. This was the Howland Great Wet Dock built by 1700 at the eastern end of the parish. Goods were not landed here, this needed to be done where customs officials were present, but the dock offered haven from bad weather and quiet water on which certain repairs could be carried out. Its facilities were tested and found to be satisfactory in the great storm of 1703. Rotherhithe also contributed to Britain's overseas expansion. The Mayflower, which carried the Pilgrim Fathers to America in 1620, was captained and part-owned by a Rotherhithe man, Christopher Jones. Other members of the crew also came from the area. In 18th century fiction Jonathan Swift's Gulliver comes from Rotherhithe.

Above top:
Old St Giles Church, Camberwell.

Above:
Bowyer Mansion House, Camberwell Road.
A watercolour of 1826 by George Yates.

Newington, Camberwell and farther south

To Southwark's south the open space of Newington and St George's Fields remained largely undeveloped. Walworth's Lord of the Manor was the Dean & Chapter of Canterbury Cathedral. The manor house, which was occupied by their lessee, was at the junction of the present Manor Place and Penton Place. In the later years of the 16th century Newington also had its own theatre. The first building at the junction of Newington Butts and the Walworth Road, a smith's shop, was built around this time. The Fishmongers' Company established an almshouse at the corner of St George's Road and Newington Butts in 1618 and the Drapers' Company founded one in 1653 at the north end of Walworth Road.

The very large parish of Camberwell extended four and a half miles north to south and two and a half east to west. It included many manors; Dulwich, Camberwell Buckingham, Friern, Colhdharbour, Milkwell, Bretynghurst, Dovedale and Basing. In character the parish was entirely rural with scattered farms and isolated settlements at Peckham, Nunhead and Dulwich. The centre of its life was the parish church of St Giles and close by was Wilson's Grammar school, founded in 1615 by the vicar, Edward Wilson. The manor house of Camberwell Buckingham was to its east at the bottom of the present Camberwell Grove and the manor house for Friern manor stood on Camberwell Road. Camberwell Buckingham was so called because the Duke of Buckingham was at one time its owner. Friern manor, which covered most of the present East Dulwich area, was owned by the Bowyer family. Later this family came to own much of the land in this area. Their manor house, Bowyer House stood until 1861. Camberwell Green is all that remains of the area's common.

Off Peckham High Street was Peckham's own manor house occupied by the Bond family. The house was pulled down in the late 17th century and rebuilt and its new gardens were praised by diarist, neighbour and garden enthusiast, John Evelyn.

Camberwell and Peckham were both the location for large fairs. Camberwell's, which in its early years lasted three weeks, was held annually at the end of August.

Dulwich was an isolated settlement farther south. It was isolated because it was away from any main highways and because it was surrounded by hills. It sense of apartness would also have been highlighted by the heavily wooded nature of much of the land around it. The meaning of its name, 'the place where the dill grew' also suggests a rural, fertile character. The foundations of modern Dulwich were laid in this period. Among Southwark's communities none have been so shaped by a single event so far back in their history. This event was the purchase, in 1605, of the manor of Dulwich by Edward Alleyn, one of the Bankside actors. Alleyn founded, in 1619, an almshouse for the poor and a school. The almshouse's

residents and the scholars were to come from places Alleyn had been associated with during his life. To fund these bodies Alleyn bequeathed them the manor and other land in the district and to this day the area has been owned and managed by Alleyns College of God's Gift, more commonly known a Dulwich College. A chapel was built in the college and this was also used by residents for their services. The burial ground at the corner of Dulwich Village and Court Lane also dates from this time.

Above:
Dulwich College.
A view of c.1750.

21

CHAPTER 5

Urbanisation: 1700-1830

The period from 1700 to the coming of the railway at the beginning of Queen Victoria's reign saw dramatic developments in, and particularly on the fringes of, the town of Southwark. The period saw these areas become part of an essentially urban, industrial whole, although some districts, such as the southern part of Walworth, were more suburban than urban in character.

One can greatly simplify London's growth and think of it as a series of concentric rings: a pulse of development taking place when circumstances were favourable, followed by periods of lesser activity. Kennington and Canonbury for example, were similar distances from the centre, developed at roughly the same time and shared, initially at least, common characteristics.

The population of the town of Southwark grew from around 35,000 in 1700 to 85,000 in 1831. An extra 74,000 could be added for the neighbouring areas of Bermondsey and Newington to which, by 1831, Southwark was inextricably joined.

This area was now firmly part of the great metropolis. All other areas were rural and agricultural with the exceptions of Rotherhithe's industrial river side and a small part of Camberwell, which developed into an exclusive suburb.

New building in north Southwark

The circumstances necessary for such dramatic expansion were complex and, among historians, the balance of factors has caused much debate. There must be a demand for land for industry and housing. This demand was powerfully provided by the London conurbation and its increasing need of goods and services. There must be capital available to finance building. There must be land available for building. Such land could only be made available when landlords were convinced that a change in use of their hitherto rural estates would be to their advantage. The most important landlords involved in Southwark's development were the City of London, who owned much of the land in the parish of St George the Martyr, and the Church (more accurately the Dean and Chapter of Canterbury), who

Left:
The Elephant & Castle. A print of c. 1800 based on a painting by Thomas Rowlandson.

Below:
The toll gate at the Dun Cow at the junction of the Old Kent Road and Upper Grange (now Dunton) Road. An anonymous early 19th century watercolour.

owned much of Walworth. Much of this land was low lying, poorly drained and largely unsuitable for building. A further prerequisite, specific to local circumstances, was the engineering skill and finance to satisfactorily drain these areas. Finally, good transport links were essential, as development would be taking place at an increasing distance from London, the river and its crossing points.

The transport factor was, in Southwark, the most visible and the most crucial. Improvements were started by the formation of the Turnpike Trusts. These were established by Parliament to manage strategic roads into London as this was a duty the parishes were failing to carry out. The Trust of the Surrey New Roads was founded in 1718 and the Bermondsey, Rotherhithe and Deptford Turnpike Trust in 1748. The former was instructed by Parliament to build Borough Road and what was later called the New Kent Road. These were laid out across open farm and common land.

The second improvement was the building of new bridges over the Thames. Until 1750, when Westminster Bridge was built, the medieval London Bridge was the only river crossing near London. Crucial for Southwark's development was the opening of Blackfriars Bridge in 1769. The bridge was promoted by the City and designed by the surveyor to the Blackfriars Bridge Committee, Robert Mylne. Its building was funded by the Bridge House Estate, an institution dating from the 12th century. Income from the land it owned (much of this in Southwark) was administered by the City and was (and is still) used for building and the upkeep of the Thames bridges into the City. Tolls were levied on those crossing until 1811.

Such a grand new bridge deserved an appropriately grand approach and various continentally-inspired road schemes were proposed to serve it and link it with other new roads, Borough Road and the New Kent Road. The scheme selected hinged on a circus on slightly higher ground in the middle of what had hitherto been Southwark's common. This was named St George's Circus recalling the parish in which it was. In 1771 an obelisk was erected at its centre.

Opposite top:
St George's Fields and The Borough in 1769 and 1797. There is considerable new building near the recently built roads across the fields

Below:
Blackfriars Bridge from a painting by William Marlow.

Above:
St George's Circus, the focal point for the new roads linking the recently built Thames bridges. The Surrey Theatre is the large building to the right.

Leading from the circus to the bridge was the impressive boulevard Great Surrey Street, now Blackfriars Road. London Road was built to connect the Circus with the Elephant & Castle.

These new roads resulted in the draining and development of much of the Christ Church area. The rebuilt Christ Church, this time on firmer foundations, was completed in 1741 but at that time it had only a small congregation to serve. This congregation was augmented by the occupants of new roads such as Charlotte Street, built by 1774, George Street and Church Street built by

1787, and all the new streets built by 1792 west of Blackfriars Road, east of Bear Lane and north of Union Street. Charlotte Street, later called Union Street was built at the request of the parish of St Saviour, which wished to gain access to the new bridge and thereby relieve congestion in Borough High Street. Other new roads radiated from St George's Circus to surrounding bridges: Waterloo Road opened in 1809 and Westminster Bridge Road in 1820. Camberwell New Road, which connected Camberwell Green and Vauxhall Bridge, opened in 1815. All were immediately heavily used.

Above top:
The Paragon, New Kent Road c.1890.

Above:
Keen's Row on the west side of the Walworth Road. Walworth's handsome buildings and rural setting are much in evidence. A watercolour of c.1779 by Richard Cuming.

St George's Fields were built on at the same time. Some of the new developments were often of a high quality such as West Square (1794). A notable later development built between 1813-40 on land owned by the Trinity House Estate was Trinity Square, south and east of St George's Church.

New building also took place in Walworth and Newington. The district's two commons, Lorrimore (meaning the lower moor, and another reminder of the marshy character of the area) and Walworth were enclosed in 1769. Much of the building that took place was promoted by Henry Penton. In 1808 Walworth Road was described as being lined with elegant mansions. Farther east at the junction of the Old and New Kent Roads was Michael Searles' Paragon (1789) and farther east again, his Surrey Square (1796). These were built on land administered by the Rolls estate, to which he was the surveyor. He lived in no 155 Old Kent Road which he built for himself. The house still stands, a grand and surprising survival close to the brutal Bricklayers Arms flyover at the north

end of the road. By the early 19th century some of Walworth's developments were starting to slip in quality. The Church, as the freeholder was unable or unwilling to regulate the builders and landlords operating on land they owned and in the face of demands for cheaper, more plentiful accommodation many new, poorer tenants moved to the area.

The Elephant & Castle is first heard of by name in 1765. Its history as a road junction is more complex and less planned than that of St George's Circus. Initially the site was simply the place where Newington Causeway divided into Newington Butts and the Walworth Road. The building of the New Kent Road linking the junction to the Old Kent Road, of St George's Road linking it to Westminster Bridge Road and of London Road linking it to St George's Circus, created a major east-west dimension. These new thoroughfares increased the value of the site and this was exploited by the founding of an inn; the Elephant & Castle. Extra pressure was placed on the Elephant & Castle junction after the opening of Southwark Bridge in 1819 and the replacement of old

Right:
Newington Butts looking south from near the Elephant & Castle. The parish church of St Mary is in the centre. A watercolour by W Hinchcliff of c.1790.

Below:
New and Old London bridges. The view is looking south towards Southwark. A painting of 1831 by George Scharf Senior

London Bridge in 1831. The new London Bridge was designed by John Rennie and built by his son, also John. It was erected about sixty yards downstream of the old. At the same time Borough High Street was realigned and widened.

Other notable improvements in communications were the building of the Surrey Canal and the Thames Tunnel. The former joined the river at Rotherhithe and, at its inception in 1801, it was intended that it should reach Portsmouth. The Rotherhithe portion, which included wider sections to accommodate docked ships, was completed in 1807. Ultimately, it went no farther than its two local termini, Addington Square, Camberwell, reached in 1811, and Canal Head, Peckham, reached in 1826. Its promoters had hoped the canal would stimulate housing and building but they were disappointed; in its early years, its presence was a boon to market gardeners and the occasional wood yard but few others.

The Thames Tunnel, which linked Rotherhithe and Wapping, is more notable as an engineering first than

for the effects it had on the area. It was the world's first underwater tunnel built by Marc and later his son Isambard Brunel. Its innovation was in the use of a tunnelling shield, a device now used in all tunnelling operations. The scheme received Parliamentary approval in 1823 but, due to financial problems, took twenty years before completion. The original plan was for the tunnel to be used by vehicular traffic but a shortage of funds prevented the building of suitable roadway access and so it remained pedestrian only until 1860. The tunnel was then taken over by the East London Railway Co. and now carries the East London Line.

Economy and society

Turning to industry and employment, the period saw the diversification and enlargement of existing industries. In Southwark, in addition to the inns, which were at their busiest, new industries arrived. Engineers were represented by John Rennie and his son, also John (later knighted), whose firm occupied premises at the Bankside end of Holland Street from 1791 for almost a century. There were early glass works at the west end of Bankside. From the early 19th century this site was given over to gas production. Prominent among brewers was Barclay Perkins' Anchor Brewery in Park Street.

It was to become London's largest brewery. Nearby was Potts' vinegar works. The Albion Mills, near Blackfriars Bridge was one of the country's first steam-powered corn mills. It aroused considerable hostility from traditional millers and was suspiciously destroyed by a fire in 1791. Encouraged by a Royal Charter granted in 1703, Bermondsey's leather industry grew; it was estimated that there were 1500 tanners in 1805. Bevingtons', to become one of the largest leather firms, opened their works on the site of a paper mill in Grange Walk in 1806.

Above left:
The Bridge and Dock House on the Surrey Canal near where it joined the River Thames at Rotherhithe. A watercolour of 1826 by George Yates.

Above centre:
The southern entrance to Brunel's Thames Tunnel in 1836. Though attractive, the illustration is more fancy than fact, as no approaches for horse-drawn traffic were ever built.

Above right:
The Albion Mills ablaze in 1791.

Right:
Jacob's Island,
Bermondsey
A watercolour of c.1880
showing a scene of
about 70 years earlier

There was a rapid growth in the populations to serve these new industries and many people lived in increasingly poor and overcrowded circumstances. Newington's population increased from 14,847 in 1801 to 44,526 in 1831 and St George the Martyr's from 22,293 in 1801 to 39,769 in 1831. Although absolute overcrowding was far from the levels reached fifty years later there were pockets of poor conditions. From 1801-1831 in the riverside parishes of the town of Southwark there were more people to the acre than in Bermondsey in 1861. Bermondsey, however, had the most notorious pocket of deprivation, Jacob's Island, an area near the riverside east of St Saviour's Dock, which had been built on from the early 18th century. There is a lack of official sources to tell us about it; investigations into social conditions were not considered to be part of the role of the authorities at of the day, so, although often repeated, Charles Dickens' description of it taken from Oliver Twist provides the most vivid picture. Looking at Folly Ditch which surrounded it he observed:

Crazy wooden galleries common to the backs of half-a-dozen houses, with holes from which to look upon the slime beneath; windows broken and patched, with poles thrust out on which to dry the linen which is never there; rooms so small, so filthy, so confined that the air would seem too tainted for even the dirt and squalor which they shelter; wooden chambers thrusting themselves out above the mud and threatening to fall in it as some have done; dirt-besmirched walls and decaying foundations; every repulsive lineament of poverty, every loathsome indication of filth, rot and garbage - all these ornament the banks of Folly Ditch... In Jacob's Island the houses have no owners, they are broken open and entered by those who have the courage; and there they live and there they die. They must have powerful motives for a secret residence, or be reduced to a destitute condition indeed, who seek a refuge in Jacob's Island.

Extraordinarily, at the heart of Jacob's Island, at the north end of George Row, stood one of Bermondsey's finest houses, the Bridge House. This was a large Dutch-style house dating from the late 17th century.

Unsurprisingly the social conditions found in Jacob's Island were accompanied by disease, although the relationship between the two was hardly noticed, let alone understood. Principal offenders against good public health were water supply and soil disposal. Water was pumped straight from the Thames, the water company having little to do other than collect bills and provide stand pipes. These were at best intermittent. There was no obligation for sewage disposal, although most human waste in the period before the invention of the water closet - night-soil, as it was euphemistically called - was collected from earth privies and was used as a fertiliser on nearby market gardens.

Southwark's reputation for lawlessness remained justified. The Clink liberty could still harbour felons and although the area known as the Mint, centred on Mint Street

in St George's parish, had its status as a sanctuary removed in 1724 it was, in the early 19th century, notorious for its atrocious housing conditions and viciousness. In *Pickwick Papers* Dickens description of it is enhanced by devastating irony:

There is a repose about Lant Street in the Borough, which sheds a gentle melancholy upon the soul... In this happy retreat are colonised a few clear-starchers, a sprinkling of journeymen bookbinders, one or wo prison agents for the Insolvent Court, several small housekeepers who are employed in the docks, a handful of mantua makers and a seasoning of jobbing tailors. The majority of inhabitants either direct their ener gies to the letting of furnished apartments or devote themselves to the healthful and invigorating pursuit of mangling...The population is migratory, usually disappearing on the verge of quarter day and generally by night. His Majesty's revenues are seldom collected in this happy valley, the rents are dubious and the water communication is very frequently cut off.

The nearby prisons and later the establishment of the Metropolitan Police were no deterrent to lawlessness. Conditions in some of the prisons were appalling, particularly in the 18th century. The Marshalsea was noteworthy. It was principally a debtor's prison whose gross overcrowding was compounded by the additional receipt of prisoners from the County courts and the Admiralty. Its administration by the Knight Marshal, a Crown official, was corrupt in the extreme. The Surrey County Justices took a more enlightened view in the building of a new jail in 1791 at Horsemonger Lane, a little south of St George's church.

Above:
The exterior of the Palace Court in the Marshalsea Prison. The prison occupied various sites along Borough High Street until it was wound up in 1842. A watercolour by J L S.

Right:
The Bethlem Hospital c.1815. The building was altered in 1835 and again in 1844-6. Part of it now houses the Imperial War Museum.

The Metropolitan Police, whose area included Southwark, was the first London-wide institution of any sort. It was founded in 1829 in the face of much opposition from the Vestries. A London-wide police force, to include the Southwark area, was first proposed in 1785. It is significant that Southwark was seen as more a part of the metropolis than of its parent county, Surrey, or the City, both of which had claims on its administration.

Many new philanthropic institutions were founded. Largest and most enduring was Guy's Hospital. This was founded in 1721 in St Thomas' Street, Southwark by Thomas Guy who was prompted by what he saw as St Thomas' Hospital's inability to cope with the demands placed on it. In 1752 Hopton's Almshouses were opened in Green Walk, later Hopton Street, Southwark. These provided for twenty six poor of the area. Many other new foundations made their home on Southwark's periphery. These included the Magdalen Hospital for Penitent Prostitutes (1768), the Philanthropic Society to Protect the Needs of the Abandoned Children of Criminals (1788) and the Bethlem Hospital. This was an ancient institution caring for the mentally ill, which in 1807 moved from the City to new, purpose-built premises on St George's fields.

The main drive in the relief of poverty and disadvantage did not come from private institutions but from a public body, the Vestries. This was the proper name for the parish-based unit of local government which had as one of its principal duties the operation of the poor law. With an increasing population inevitably came poverty, and workhouses, where the poor were given very basic lodging as a reward for work, were built by many of the parishes. The St George the Martyr workhouse was in Mint Street and the St Saviour's workhouse was a little to its west.

Southwark was also home to a pioneering educational institution. This was to become the British & Foreign Schools Society, which was founded on Borough Road in 1806 by Joseph Lancaster. Its innovation was twofold; the monitorial system whereby large numbers of children could be effectively taught, and the fact that it was non-sectarian. The country's first deaf-and-dumb school was founded in Bermondsey in 1792 and the School for the Indigent Blind at St George's Circus in 1802.

Above:
Southwark Fair after a print of 1735 by William Hogarth.

Above right:
An artist's impression of the planned music hall at the Surrey Gardens. It was erected in 1856.
After a fire in 1861 it was rebuilt, and between 1862 and 1871 housed the displaced St Thomas' Hospital.

Right:
Queen Victoria and Prince Albert visiting the Surrey Zoological Gardens in 1848.

The area was home to a number of noted fairs and entertainments, some long established, others new. Southwark Fair dated from the medieval period but had its heyday in the 18th century. It was held during September, occupied an increasingly large site at the south end of the high street and lasted fourteen days. Because of the congestion it caused it was closed in 1756. A new market, independent of the City, was established in 1757 on a site known as the triangle, south of the Cathedral and west of the High Street. This is the origin of the modern wholesale fruit and vegetable market.

The 18th century saw a vogue for the medicinal properties of spa water and a number of spas opened taking advantage of plentiful supplies of clean water, open space and easy access to London. The Dog & Duck was one, operating from 1730-99 in St George's Fields and Bermondsey Spa, founded in 1780 and operated by Thomas Keyse, was another. Both incorporated other features including tea gardens, art galleries and musical attractions. Walworth at one time had a rival to Regent's Park Zoo in

the form of Edward Cross' Royal Surrey Zoological Gardens, which occupied a site near Manor Place from 1831 to 1856. The Montpelier Cricket Club used to meet at the Beehive Tea Gardens at the present Carter Street in Walworth, until it moved to the Oval in 1844 as the foundation of the Surrey Cricket Club.

The spiritual needs of the new populations were most rapidly provided for by the nonconformist churches. A very early example was the Zoar Street Chapel in Southwark dating from 1687 and later examples were the York Street Chapel in Newington built in 1790 and the Southwark Chapel in Long Lane. The Surrey Chapel on Blackfriars Road was founded in 1782 and the preacher, Rowland Hill, attracted large congregations. The building was last used for services in 1881 and was converted first into a theatre and later a boxing ring.

After the relaxation of laws that had previously restricted their ability to worship freely, the Roman Catholics from 1788 opened a series of temporary chapels in the St George's Fields area. These catered for the immigrant Irish community.

The Anglicans were slowest to respond to the increase in population but did so with new church buildings of great style. Noteworthy examples are Holy Trinity, Trinity Church Square by Francis Bedford, opened 1824, St James' Thurland Road in Bermondsey designed by James Savage and opened in 1829 and St Peter's Walworth designed by John Soane and opened in 1825.

Rotherhithe stands apart from these developments both geographically and economically. Apart from along the river front, it was still separated from Bermondsey by fields and market gardens bounded by water-filled ditches. For much of this period Rotherhithe was known as Redriff, an abbreviated form of its name. Its 1831 population was a relatively small 13,000 living in streets close to St Mary's church.

The area was inextricably tied to the river and the sea. In the late 18th century the Howland dock was renamed the Greenland to reflect its use by the whaling trade and in 1807 the Commercial Dock Company was formed. This started the modern development of the docks. New docks were built and by 1820 the acreage of water had increased to 50; a five fold increase since 1802 when work started on the canal. The trades

in timber and grain, to become prominent in the later 19th century, were established.

Shipbuilding yards were busy particularly with Royal Naval orders during periods of war and work for the East India Company at other times. Repairers' and breakers' yards were also important, most famously the one run by John Beatson who broke up the Bellepheron, the vessel that carried Napoleon to exile and the Temeraire, a veteran of Trafalgar and subject of Turner's famous painting. Beatson's premises were adjacent to the Surrey Lock, the entrance to the canal.

By 1700 the parish church, St Mary's, was in a poor state of repair, a situation made worse by a flood five

Left:
A floating dock at Rotherhithe c. 1820

Below left:
The Fighting Temeraire being towed to Beatson's yard in Rotherhithe to be broken up. Turner's painting of c.1838. The details of both the Temeraire, and the tug are not correct.

Right:
The residence of William de Crespigny at Denmark Hill. Numerous grand houses of this sort were built in Denmark Hill at the end of the 18th century. A watercolour of 1827.

years later. The parish's request to the government for money for a new building from the coal tax-funded Fifty New Churches Act was rejected. A new church was built in 1714-15, funded by voluntary donations.

Camberwell and farther south

The huge Camberwell parish was almost entirely rural as late as 1831 although its population was starting to increase rapidly. In 1801 it was 7,000 but it quadrupled in the next 30 years. The parish was made up of four settlements; the largest, Camberwell proper; Peckham to its east; the hamlet of Nunhead to Peckham's south east, and Dulwich in the south. By 1830 Camberwell proper had two distinct

areas. North of Church Street and Peckham Road there were houses along Camberwell Road linking it to the developments farther north in Walworth. Many of these new houses were large and of some quality. There were also numerous streets of smaller houses such as those on Albany Road and Southampton Way. There was also ribbon development along the Old Kent Road. South of Church Street were developments of an altogether different order. These owed their origin to the sale, in 1776, of the manor of Camberwell Buckingham and the demolition of the manor house, which stood on the south side of Church Street just east of the church. This gave access to an hitherto private road lined by an avenue of trees. This became Camberwell Grove and it was rapidly developed with grand mansions at its northern end. Camberwell was seen as an attractive place to settle; its higher ground provided fresher air and its wells a plentiful supply of clean water. A new species of butterfly was sighted for the first time in the area and was named the Camberwell Beauty. The Champion Hill area was developed in the 1790s and the area at the south

end of Camberwell Grove after 1810 when the eminent Doctor, John Coakley Lettsom, who had been a resident since 1779, sold his estate.

Peckham was altogether more rural. Its open spaces provided pasture for animals being driven to the London markets and, later, especially after the building of the canal, fertile land for market gardening. Peckham also had its up-market aspect with large houses occupied by the wealthy. Most notable was Peckham House, which stood south of Peckham Road on the site occupied by Warwick Park School and occupied by the Spitta family until 1826.

Dulwich became the most desirable place for the wealthy to settle, especially after its commons, were enclosed in 1805 and 1808. College Road, which was extended south in 1787, and Dulwich Common still contain many houses dating from this period. The most striking surviving example is Belair, built in 1785 for John Willes, a merchant. The house was originally called College Place. Bell House on College Road dating from 1767 is another example.

Houses on the newly enclosed common included Glenlea designed by the surveyor to the College, George Tappen. A number of the grand houses no longer stand. These include a mansion built in 1795 for Lord Thurlow, the Lord Chancellor and Hall Place, the ancient manor house which stood to the west of the village near the present Park Hall Road. It was demolished in 1880.

Dulwich also developed as a centre or recreation and entertainment. Popular diversions were provided by the Dulwich Spa of John Cox. From about 1704 he provided access through the newly cut woodland walk that still bears his name, from his inn, the Green Man (the site of the present Grove Tavern) to the spa at Sydenham Wells. In 1739 his son dug a well and discovered a mineral spring beneath their inn so saving their visitors a walk and making himself wealthy.

Dulwich Picture Gallery, which was owned and run by the College, attracted a rather different visitor, but, since a condition of the grant of money for its building was that its should be open to the public, it has been, as accessible as the most popular tavern. It was opened in 1817. The picture collection, originally owned by Noel Desenfans, was left to Dulwich College by his friend Sir Francis Bourgeois. Desenfans' wife, Margaret gave money for the erection of the gallery. It was designed by Sir John Soane. The collection was added to by pictures already owned by the College and more recently by bequest and purchase.

Below left:
Dulwich Picture Gallery. A view of 1826 by George Yates.

Below:
Heaton's Folly in Peckham. Heaton's Folly stood just south of Queen's Road. It was built in the 1790s by Mr Heaton simply to provide productive work for the unemployed of the day. A watercolour by J B Cuming.

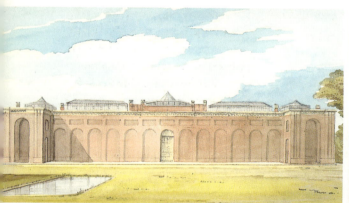

CHAPTER 6

Suburbanisation: The Parish of Camberwell, 1830-1900

While the period before Queen Victoria's accession saw the extension of the town of Southwark and part of the parish of Bermondsey south into their hitherto rural hinterland, the period of her reign saw the development of much of the rest of the present borough. With the exception of Dulwich, a great deal of the huge Camberwell parish was developed by 1900.

The term suburb was reinvented by the Victorians and applied to developments we would today recognise as suburban: a district some way from the city centre in which many of the suburb's residents worked; a planned development of houses of contemporary but conservative character, populated by residents who were, or considered themselves to be, of a higher social status than those they had left behind in the inner-city. In one sense areas of Southwark were already suburbs well before the Victorian period. Much of Walworth, Peckham, occasional smart developments off the Old Kent Road and, most spectacularly, Camberwell Grove and Grove Lane, were suburban.

Before considering the Camberwell area in detail, it will be worthwhile to consider the sources for the Victorian period as a whole. These sources become richer as the period progresses. This was largely a result of the increasing inquisitiveness of government, whose starting point for their limited forays in social activity was the gathering of information. However, other factors assisted the increasing number of sources: technology, changes in taxation and the developing role of those outside government in providing social relief.

Technology produced cheap, wood-based paper and a printing industry, which developed particularly strong roots in Southwark. Novels, periodicals such as the *Illustrated London News* and *The Builder*, local newspapers, (which started in Southwark from 1855), and publications concerning commerce and manufacturing, particularly the Kelly's London Trade directories, produced annually from 1841, were all produced in quantity. The records of government, local, metropolitan and national, became fuller and more widely available. 1870 saw the first comprehensive and detailed large scale mapping of the metropolitan area; this, and succeeding surveys provide a detailed and easy to understand picture of the changing city. A second invention was photography and the area was of interest to many photographers. Printing was also encouraged by fiscal measures: the abolition of the stamp duty on newspapers and of taxes on paper.

The pioneers of social inquisitiveness produced documents more accessible but no less shocking than their government counterparts. Henry Mayhew's *London Labour and the London Poor* (1851), Charles Booth's *Life and Labour of the People in London* (1889) and accompanying map, which classifies the social status of the occupants of each street, and George Dodd's *Days at the factories* (1843), which describes London's industrial processes, are all indispensable. Also important is Charles Dickens who used Southwark as the setting of many of his novels and who made more of the country aware of the horrors of metropolitan life than any newspaper editor or civil servant.

New building

By the 1830s, due to the expansion in manufacturing activity, some of Southwark's early suburbs were being relieved of their previously desirable status; respectable residents were being driven out by the increasing subdivision of large houses into smaller units and their occupation by those seeking work, often casual in nature, in developing industry to the north. These displaced residents looked to the south for new accommodation.

By 1830 little of the area south of Peckham Road had been built on, the exceptions being around Camberwell

Grove, in Dulwich Village, along Rye Lane (then called South Street) and along the north side of the Rye itself. By contrast, development farther north was more intensive with ribbon developments along the Old Kent Road, Camberwell Road, Hill Street and Peckham Road, and also in the area around Southampton Street (now Southampton Way).

In the early years of Victoria's reign Camberwell was certainly a fashionable place to live. It was home to many who moved away from the City or West-End and had the time and money to commute to their work. One such family were the Chamberlains; their son Joseph, later politician and statesman, was born in 1836 in Camberwell Grove. Another famous resident was John Ruskin, the artist, writer and thinker, who lived for a time in Herne Hill and then from 1842 to 1872 at 163 Denmark Hill. This house became a gathering place for many of the leading intellectuals of the day. Robert Browning, the author, also spent his early years in the area, living, until 1840, in Southampton Street.

A whole range of services developed to cater for these wealthy residents: private schools, such as the Denmark Hill Grammar School or the Camberwell Collegiate School for Boys, or new churches. St George's Wells Way was built in 1824 for the new residents of the grand terraces on Camberwell Road and St Giles', the ancient parish church, was completely rebuilt in 1844 after a fire three years earlier. Its size and self-confidence reflect the character of the area at the time. There were also many long-established nonconformist churches, such as Grove Chapel (on Camberwell Grove) founded in 1819.

Such exclusivity did not remain widespread, nor did it last. Between 1840 and 1870 major changes took place north of Peckham Road. The area, only partly developed in 1840, was to be fully built in the next thirty years. Although not uniform in character, many of the later houses, and particular those west of the canal, were of a lower standard than those of earlier years. This whole area suffered a period of social decay in subsequent years most extremely in the area around Sultan Street to the west of Camberwell Road. Industry also came to this area; prominent was the South Metropolitan Gas Works on the Old Kent Road.

In 1841 the population of the whole of Camberwell parish was 40,000, in 1871 111,000 and in 1891, 235,000. The area north of Peckham Road saw its most dramatic rate of growth in

Opposite top:
St George's Church, Wells Way. A watercolour of 1827.

Opposite bottom:
Denmark Hill showing one of the typically fine mansions built in the area. In the foreground is the Camberwell omnibus. A line drawing and wash of c.1800.

Right:
The South Metropolitan Gas Works on the Old Kent Road. A postcard of c.1900

Above:
East Dulwich in maps of c1870
and c.1895 showing the very rapid
development of the area.

the years before 1871 (it doubled its population between 1851 and 1871) while areas farther south grew most swiftly between 1871 and 1885.

This second pulse of building took place after 1870 and in three broad areas: north of East Dulwich Station; in Nunhead, south of Queen's Road but north of Evelina Road and a huge area in East Dulwich to the east of Lordship Lane. The East Dulwich development was carried out by the British Land Company who had bought the Friern Manor farm from the Bowyer Smyth family and then sold building leases to building firms, who took the actual risk of constructing new houses. Despite construction by many builders and over a fairly long period, the houses of this development were of a fairly uniform size and character, typically two-storied brick terrace with a bay window. They attracted a new population from aspiring working-classes including a high proportion employed in clerical activities.

The population of East Dulwich and the surrounding district grew from 31,000 in 1871 to 82,000 twenty years later. Many factors influenced the pace of this development but crucially the availability of capital determined when houses were built and transport when they were tenanted. Thus, many new houses were built during the capital-fuelled building boom of 1878-80 but remained empty until after the introduction of cheaper rail fares about five years later.

The final large pulse of building took place in the late 1880s when the area south-east of Nunhead cemetery was developed by Edward Yates as the Waverley Estate. In character it was even more uniform than East Dulwich and populated by similar tenants.

Transport

Much of this change can be attributed to the arrival of new forms of transport: railways, horse buses and horse trams. These provided the new, largely middle-class and upper working-class, residents affordable, reliable and quick transport to their places of work.

The railways arrived from the 1860s. The London Chatham & Dover's line from the Elephant & Castle to Herne Hill via Camberwell was built in 1862. On the South Eastern's line to Bromley South and Dover, Dulwich (later West Dulwich) and Sydenham Hill stations were opened in 1863. The London Brighton & South Coast's loop from London Bridge to Victoria via South Bermondsey, Queens Road, Peckham Rye and Denmark Hill stations was built in 1867, and the South London and Sutton's line of 1868, which linked Peckham Rye and Sutton, saw the building of East and North Dulwich stations. Of Southwark's present stations, the final one to be opened was Nunhead in 1871; this was a staging post on the Chatham's so-called high-level line to Crystal Palace via Honor Oak and Lordship Lane, which had been opened six years earlier. Nunhead was also a kick off point for the Chatham's line to Greenwich Park. Both lines were unsuccessful: the Crystal Palace line finally closed in 1954 and the Greenwich Park line in 1917. Until the introduction of workmen's fares in the mid 1880s the railways' fares were beyond the reach of most ordinary workers and the lines were operating well short of their capacity.

Above:
A Thomas Tilling horse bus outside
Nunhead Station in c.1905.

Road transport also played its part.
New roads were built such as East
Dulwich Grove in the late 1870s,
or existing ones widened, such as
Camberwell Church Street, or
Peckham Road. Horse buses were in
operation from 1851 when Thomas
Tilling started his service from
Peckham Rye to the City. Like the
railways, they served principally the
populations south of Peckham Road.
Bus services were to be outstripped in
capacity, frequency and cost (but not
coverage) by the arrival of the trams.

Tram lines were built along
Camberwell and Peckham Roads in
the early 1870s. These provided
transport to an already resident but,
compared to those farther south,
poorer, population living north of
Peckham Road, a population that had
never been able to afford it before.

One area of the parish of
Camberwell that remained untouched
by these momentous changes was
Dulwich. Events (or lack of them)
here illustrate how the absence of
just one of the factors necessary for
development (in this case a landlord
willing to let building leases) utterly
prevented any change despite the
obvious presence of other factors
(transport, capital and expanding
population). The 1450 acres that
made up the Dulwich estate
were managed by the estate governors
to provide an income to the schools
and other local charities. They
attempted to do this by allowing
only building that would be attractive
to the wealthy, upper-middle-class
and professional parents of potential
pupils. Thus the small amount of
building that was allowed in the very
last years of the 19th century was

strictly regulated in terms of its size (large detached houses) and location (near the boundaries of the estate). So successful were the Dulwich estate governors in controlling development that, in 1901, Dulwich had the lowest population density anywhere in London, save Eltham.

Social conditions

While the building of suburban Camberwell was preceded by a transport infrastructure, most other services and amenities arrived considerably after the new residents. Utilities were provided privately: sewers by the developer under the eye of the Metropolitan Board of Works and gas by the South Metropolitan Gas Company, although it was not until the 1890s, when pre-payment

meters were introduced, that its use came within reach of the majority. The needs of the poor were addressed by the Board of Guardians as established by the 1834 Poor Law Reform Act. The aim of this Act was to do away with the perceived leniency and maladministration of the parish-based system. However in Camberwell things carried on much as before; the Board of Guardians administered the same geographical area as the parish and they continued to give out (i.e. outside of the

workhouse) relief to the destitute. Not all social relief was provided by official bodies as, for example, in 1889 the Cambridge House Settlement was founded. Based on Camberwell Road, this organisation was run by conscientious members of Cambridge University who provided activities and assistance to the disadvantaged of the area. The Licensed Victuallers established in 1828 an almshouse in Asylum Road, Peckham for retired members of their trade. The striking classical building still stands.

Since Elizabethan times the parish, as well as maintaining its church, had, through the Vestry, also been the basis for the civil administration of the area. These Vestries were reformed in 1856 and among their new responsibilities were roads, (rudimentary) public health inspection, the burial of the dead and building inspections. Further powers were added later: slum clearance and the provision of housing, libraries and open spaces. Many of these powers were discretionary, thus, the Sultan Street slums were hardly interfered with, while, on the other hand, open spaces were safeguarded most notably by the purchase in 1868

of Peckham Rye, Goose Green and Nunhead Green. One Tree Hill only came into public hands after its highly unpopular enclosure by a golf club in 1896. This led to its occupation by residents and eventual purchase by the Camberwell authorities in 1902. Dulwich Park came into the London County Council's hands not only to safeguard the space from development but also as a gift from the College who wished to provide a buffer between its exclusive population to the park's south and the working-classes to its north in East Dulwich. Dulwich Baths at Goose Green opened in 1892. Dulwich Library opened in 1897.

Education, such as it existed for the masses, had largely been provided through the churches or the Ragged School Union, but, in 1870, the London School Board was established and its huge, barrack-like buildings - warehouses for education - started to appear, the only buildings to puncture the skyline other than churches and chimneys. Twelve were built in Camberwell by 1880. The education provision made by Dulwich College, though a world away from the aspiration of universal free elementary education, underwent equally momentous change in the mid-19th century. One change was prompted by

Below left:
Brown's Farm, Peckham Rye. A watercolour of 1818 by J B Cuming.

Below:
The church of St John the Evangelist, Goose Green East Dulwich. One of the finer and most attractively located of the many Victorian churches built in the area.

Brown's Farm, Peckham Rye.

Camberwell's Anglican churches were augmented by, for example, St Paul's, Herne Hill, of 1844 and rebuilt 1858, St John's, Goose Green, of 1865, and St Peter's Lordship Lane, of 1869, designed by Charles Barry.

Increasing leisure time, a phenomenon that grew towards the end of the century, was filled by new diversions. While Camberwell fair finally closed in 1868, music halls, such as the Camberwell Palace of Varieties on Denmark Hill, or many of the over 300 pubs were no less lively. The South London Fine Art Gallery on Peckham Road opened in 1891. It was founded by William Rossiter and part financed by the philanthropist Passmore Edwards. It was unusually welcoming in its approach and in 1896 it came under the Vestry's control. Societies such as the Peckham Improvement Society provided for the energetic of mind, while sporting clubs such as Peckham Hare & Hounds, (later to evolve into Blackheath Harriers), founded in 1869, provided for the energetic of body. In the very last years of the century cycling became hugely fashionable and the Herne Hill cycle

track opened in 1896 to provide for those of a competitive nature.

Retail shops developed from the mid-Victorian period. There were main shopping streets in Lordship Lane, Denmark Hill, Camberwell Church Street and Rye Lane. On the last were some of the most famous names in south London shopping, notably Holdrons and Jones & Higgins, which was founded in 1867.

an Act of 1857 which reformed the College into upper and lower schools. This was followed by much vigorous improvement by the new headmaster. Also refounded around this time was James Allen's Girls' School which moved to its present premises in 1886. The second development was the provision of extravagant new buildings for Dulwich College. These were designed in a flamboyant Italianate style by Charles Barry the younger and funded by money raised from the sale of estate land to the railway company. The College originally intended that these would house both the upper and lower schools but rising numbers made this impossible. In 1882 the lower school became Alleyn's School and it moved to new premises in 1887.

Above:
Dulwich College as rebuilt to designs by Charles Barry in 1870.
Right:
An advertisement for pedal cycle racing at Herne Hill Track in 1893.

CHAPTER 7

A city ignored: Southwark, Bermondsey and Rotherhithe, 1830-1900

The established and increasingly industrialised communities of Southwark, Bermondsey, Rotherhithe and north Camberwell were a world away from the modestly comfortable clerks of Nunhead, let alone Dulwich's wealthy merchants and professionals. On, and near, the riverside was to be found an existence in large part nasty, brutal and short. It was one where the needs of people, if ever considered, were subsumed to the imperative of expanding manufacturing, commerce and transport.

The seventy years to 1900 saw massive changes to north Southwark's townscape. All available space was occupied by industry, transport or housing. Behind the grand houses lining the main roads were no longer fields but streets of meaner, crowded dwellings and the last remaining spaces of open riverfront were taken by multi-storey grey brick warehouses.

The big themes of Victorian Southwark were industry, transport and social conditions. One third of London's population was employed in manufacturing, making it the country's most important centre.

Above:
Barclay Perkins' Anchor Brewery in Park Street in 1841.

Industry

Southwark, Bermondsey and Rotherhithe provided a suitable location for industry. The river allowed the easy transport of bulky raw materials, there was a plentiful supply of cheap labour, and the area was close to London, the destination of many of the goods. However, the district lacked extensive open spaces so factories were squeezed in as and when land became available. As early as 1871 the population of riverside Southwark began to fall, but the pressure on land for industrial purposes meant that the population became no less densely packed.

Different areas of London had different industries. Southwark's particular specialisms were hat making, iron founding and brewing. In 1895, the silk hat trade employed approximately 1500. In the early Victorian period felt hats were important, those involved in their manufacture being gradually poisoned by the vapours of dilute sulphuric acid used to mould the mass of felt into the fashion of the day. Beaver hats were also coveted luxury items and Christy's in Bermondsey Street was, in 1843, reputed to be the world's largest manufacturer. Another industry concentrated in Southwark was printing and, as with hat making, there was a large number of small firms.

The rebuilding carried out at Barclay Perkins' Anchor Brewery in Park Street after a fire in 1833 made it the largest in London. Together with smaller breweries and the area's easy access from Kent, Southwark became the centre for England's hop trade. Many firms, such as Wood, Hanbury, Bevan & Jackson, sold hops, and in 1867, in the newly built Southwark Street, the flamboyant Hop Exchange was erected; a worthy rival to any of the City's commodity exchanges. The Borough Market, governed from the mid-18th century by independent trustees, served as Southwark's wholesale and retail market (the retail functions were not dropped until the early years of the 20th century). Southwark's oldest surviving provisions dealer is J Sainsbury, who moved to the area in 1869.

Iron founders and engineers represented heavy manufacturing industry. John Rennie's works have been discussed in a previous chapter, but there were others: the engineers, Easton, Amos and Anderson, had premises in Ewer Street until c.1887; Stevens, in Southwark Bridge Road made railway signals. Other firms were Haywards, whose sign of the dog and pot was used on coal-hole covers, Cole's cranes in Sumner Street and Willcox in Southwark Street.

Bermondsey was most noted for two industries, food and leather. A large proportion of London's imported foodstuffs were landed at its wharves indeed Tooley Street claimed the title of London's larder and so it is not surprising that food manufacturers became established.

The largest wharfinger was the Hay's Wharf Company on Tooley Street. The firm dated back to the 17th century, but it greatly improved its facilities in the mid 19th century principally, in 1856 by building a new dock into its riverside warehouses (rebuilt after the Tooley Street fire of 1861). The company handled a wide variety of foodstuffs such as China tea or products from Britain's colonies.

Food and drink manufacturers were abundant in the area, perfuming the air with a cocktail of smells. Pungent odours came from Sarson's Vinegar factory in Tower Bridge Road and from Crosse & Blackwell's pickles in Crimscott Street; the smell of malt came from Courage's Anchor Brewery in Horselydown Lane. Sweet and cloying smells came from Pearce & Duff's custard powder factory in Spa Road, Shuttleworth's chocolates in Galleywall Road and Hartley's jams in Tower Bridge Road. The largest food factory was Peak, Frean & Co. Peek, Frean was founded in 1857 by James Peek and George Hender Frean. Business expanded especially after the introduction of new, more palatable and better textured biscuits. In 1866 the firm moved from their original premises at Dockhead, Bermondsey to a new 10 acre site next to the railway. This factory, in Drummond Road, was to be their home for more than one hundred years. Most of those who worked in the food processing factories were women. The Bermondsey factory girls had a deserved reputation for boisterous and often coarse behaviour.

Left:
Hay's Wharf showing the arrival of the tea clipper, the *Flying Spur*, in 1862. An oil painting by Gordon Ellis.

Tea was prominent in the mid-Victorian period but, with the introduction of refrigeration, which the company pioneered, so was New Zealand dairy produce, which arrived from 1867, and meat from 1879. Many of the sturdy and solemn warehouses so characteristic of London's industrial riverside date from the mid and late 19th century. The Home and Foreign Produce Exchange was established in 1886 near Tooley Street thus asserting Southwark's dominance over the City in this field.

While the Hay's Wharf Company pioneered food storage facilities at the wholesale end of the trade, Bryan Donkin did so at the retail end with his introduction into Britain of the process for tinning food. His factory stood in Grange Road from 1811.

By contrast, the Bermondsey leather industry produced smells few would wish to recall. Skins from all manner of animals - cattle, sheep, pigs, goats and oxen - were cured in the numerous leather works in the area. Each type of skin was cured in a different way depending on its final intended use. Leather could be prepared in four ways: by oak bark which produced stout leather from large animals; by sumach, (a vegetable based cure) used to make morocco leather (which has a glossy finish) from goat skins; by alum, used to make soft, kid leather from sheep or goat hides, and by oil, used to produce chamois or wash-leathers. As each stage in the process called for different skills, the trade was sub-divided into jealously guarded specialisms.

The largest works in the district were those of Barrow, Hepburn & Gale and of Bevingtons' whose works at the Neckinger Mills in Grange Road in the late 19th century produced half a million cured skins each year. Just as a food exchange was established on Tooley Street, so was a leather Market built by 1830 in Weston Street.

Nearly all of Rotherhithe's economy was devoted to activities associated with the river. Exceptions were Brandram's paint factory in the Lower Road, the gas works to the east end of the built up area of the town and a number of manure works, some, to the distress of residents, inland, away from the river's air-clearing breeze.

Above: Bevingtons' Neckinger Leather Mills in 1862.

Left: Bermondsey factory girls fighting. The picture is from a report on the social and moral conditions of the area prepared by the parish of St Mary Magdalen in 1896. The report's negative comments on the district and its population incurred the wrath of the Vestry.

Central to Rotherhithe's economy were the docks which expanded after the amalgamation in 1865 of the two rival companies into the Surrey Commercial Dock Company. In 1876 the Canada Dock was completed bringing the total extent of the docks to 176 acres of water and five miles of quayside. An important feature of the work of the dock and wharves were the lighters, small unpowered barges piloted by skilled operators who transferred goods from ship to shore. Many Thames Lightermen lived in Bermondsey and they were among the area's working-class elite. Equally skilled were the distinctive porters who worked in the Surrey Docks' timber trade. These were the deal porters who, with panache, carried and stacked lengths of timber.

Shipbuilding, repairing and breaking were also important to Rotherhithe's economy. There were about a dozen yards in operation; typically they occupied a wharf or small dock on the riverside of Rotherhithe Street with maybe a storage area on the other. Various types of vessels were built, from tea clippers such as the

Left:
The building of the Canada Dock in 1875. From a photograph by Morgan & Lang

Bottom left:
Norway Dock in the foreground, looking towards Lady Dock and Acorn Pond. A photograph of 1875.

Lothair of 1870, to an early iron steamboat, the *Aaron Manby*, which had its pre-fabricated sections assembled here in 1822.

Rotherhithe and Bermondsey, at least in the early and middle Victorian period, were not entirely industrial as much of their open space, the area bounded to the north and east by Jamaica Road and the Lower Road and to the south by the Old Kent Road and the canal, was given over to market gardening.

Most of those who worked these industries were employed on a casual basis and paid for piece-work. This gave the employers the flexibility they required and ensured that their workforce did not become too organised. Despite this lack of organisation, the Surrey Docks were seriously disrupted for five weeks during the strike for better wages in 1889. Casual employment meant incomes were irregular, hours long and, in the absence of cheap public transport, people were forced to live in grossly overcrowded conditions near their sources of work. This overcrowding was made worse as

landlords made greater profits from land put to industrial, as opposed to residential use.

As industries grew, so did populations. The figure for Southwark, Bermondsey, Rotherhithe and Newington combined grew from 179,000 in 1831 to 276,000 in 1861 (a 55% increase) and to 337,000 in 1900, (a 23% increase on 1861 and a 92% increase on 1831). The fastest rate of growth was in the early Victorian period and in the outer parishes of Bermondsey, Rotherhithe and Newington. Bermondsey's population all but doubled from 30,000 in 1831 to 58,000 in 1861, Rotherhithe's increased by a similar amount (13,000 in 1831 to 24,000 in 1861) and Newington's from 45,000 to 82,000 in the same period. Growth continued, but more slowly up to 1901: their respective totals then were 82,000, 38,000 and 122,000, a 47% increase. Conversely, the total for the much smaller riverside parishes of the town of Southwark (Christ Church, St John Horselydown, St Olave, St Thomas and St Saviour) fell, from a peak of 55,000 in 1861, to 34,000 in 1901.

Approximately one third of these new populations were attributable to a natural increase of the existing population and approximately two thirds to immigration. People came to the area from two main sources. Most came in a fairly even spread from southern England and the west country but there was also a sizeable community of Irish, measurable in thousands. They were particularly concentrated in Bermondsey and St George's Fields. Many came to work on the new London and Greenwich Railway, which was built in the mid-1830s, and their numbers were swelled again by the Irish famine of the late-1840s.

More revealing again are the population densities, the number of people to the acre. In 1831 the figure for Bermondsey was 47, for Newington, 70 and for Rotherhithe, 31 (the Rotherhithe figure has been calculated excluding the acreage of the docks from the total area of the parish). The corresponding figures for 1861 are 93 for Bermondsey, 130 for Newington and 60 for Rotherhithe; the London average in 1861 was 30. In 1900 there were 131 persons to the acre in Bermondsey, 193 in Newington and 94 in Rotherhithe. In the town of Southwark overcrowding was more acute and longer established. It had 150 persons to the acre in 1831 and 167 in 1861. This acute overcrowding had a huge impact on public health.

Transport

Railways have a very different place in Southwark's history than in Camberwell's. London Bridge became enshrined in railway history as London's first permanent railway terminus and some of the boldest railway extensions took place through Southwark's overcrowded streets.

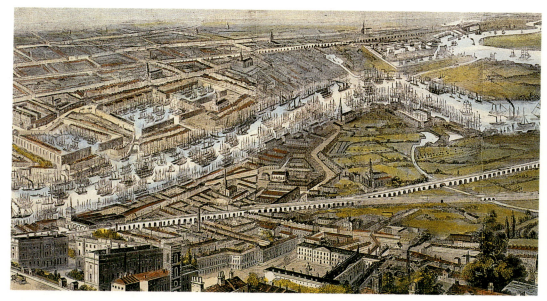

London's first railway, the London and Greenwich, ran through Rotherhithe and Bermondsey and ended at London's first, but temporary, railway terminus at Spa Road, Bermondsey. The line was opened in 1836 and was extended later that year to London Bridge. The first station buildings did not appear until 1841. The line was built through largely open country and was carried on a viaduct of 878 brick arches. In 1839 the London and Croydon Railway was built and in 1841 the London and Brighton. These

two companies amalgamated in 1846. Their lines departed from those of the London and Greenwich at the Corbett's Lane junction and this necessitated the building of the world's first signal box. The South Eastern (or Dover) Railway opened a route to Dover in 1842 and Gravesend in 1849. In an attempt to avoid the tolls of the London and Greenwich line and to rival and usurp their terminus at London Bridge, the London and Croydon and the South Eastern promoted an alternative new terminus just to the north of the

Old Kent Road in Bermondsey. This was called the Bricklayers' Arms after an inn on the nearby road. Passenger services continued only to 1852 after which time the depot was used only for freight.

Initially the railway's impact on the locality was limited to the visual and aural impact of a massive structure carrying vehicles powered by radically new technology. In its early days it caused no great shifts of population but it did have a profound effect on the inns of Borough High Street whose

Opposite left:
A panorama of the
River Thames by
Smith, 1845. Prominent
are the London &
Greenwich Railway and
a busy River Thames.

Above:
The viaduct of the
London & Greenwich
Railway drawn prior to
construction in 1833.

business was severely damaged by this new, swifter means of transport.

A second phase of railway building occurred in the 1860s. South from existing termini went all existing lines through the southern part of the present borough. Their building has been discussed in the previous chapter. The building of railway extensions in the opposite direction, from established termini farther into the City and the West End, had an equally profound, but entirely negative impact on the resident population. In 1864 the London Chatham and Dover extended their line from its terminus at the Elephant & Castle to Blackfriars and in 1859 the Charing Cross Railway Company, a subsidiary of the South Eastern, gained permission to extend west from London Bridge to Charing Cross. The disruption brought by this line, along with the slightly later spur to Cannon Street, must rank with the other great destructive incidents in Southwark's history, the fires of the 17th century and the blitz of the 20th.

There were two great casualties of the extension to Charing Cross: St Thomas' Hospital and the homes of approximately 8,000 people. St Thomas' Hospital strenuously opposed the Act that gave permission for the building of the line and took the company to court in attempts to improve the offer of compensation and to delay the start of work. They lost and the hospital moved from the site they had occupied for over 600 years to temporary, unsatisfactory, accommodation in vacant buildings that had housed the Royal Surrey Zoo in Manor Place, Walworth. There they stayed until 1871 when their new premises were built on the Lambeth riverfront, just south of Westminster Bridge. The Borough Market, though disadvantaged by the building of the railway viaduct immediately above its roof, continued trading defiantly.

It has been estimated that up to 40,000 people were displaced during the first 25 years of railway building in inner South London. By far the single biggest portion of this number was affected by the Charing Cross extension. The official figure was 4,500, though the actual one has been estimated at

8,000. The railway company was required to pay no compensation and used the specious argument that the displaced populations could live in new houses and commute to work on the railway that had just made them homeless. This argument conveniently ignored the facts that most work was casual, so necessitating a home very close to potential employers, the extreme length of the working day and the prohibitive cost of the fares. In 1861 the South Eastern Railway built at London Bridge a grand new hotel which remained largely unoccupied until 1893, when it was converted into the Company's offices.

To the dismay of the railway companies and their investors, many railway lines were working below capacity in the 1870s and it was not until the Cheap Trains Act of 1883, which gave the Board of Trade power to require companies to charge fares within the workman's budget, that the lines built in the 1860s started to work close to capacity.

The final addition to the complement of railway lines was considerably less visible, the underground railways.

Underground lines were slow to come south of the river, partly due to the existing above ground coverage, and partly due to difficult geology. The City and South London Railway opened its line from King William Street to Stockwell via London Bridge, Borough and the Elephant & Castle in 1890. It was the world's first electric tube railway.

Road transport, both its infrastructure and services, also developed greatly during the Victorian period. Cross-

river journeys were made easier by the abolition of bridge tolls and the later building of a new Blackfriars Bridge in 1869. The most prominent improvement was the building of another new bridge over the river, Tower Bridge. The need for a new bridge downstream of London Bridge had been recognised as early as 1879 but the Act authorising it was not passed until 1885. The design had to meet two main criteria: to allow the passage of large ships (a minimum open span of 200 feet and height of

Below left:
The extension of the railway from London Bridge to the City and the West End. This was one of the most destructive events in Southwark's history. A view of 1863.

Right:
Tower Bridge under construction. A view of 24 September 1892.

135 feet was specified) and to be in the Gothic style. The architect was Sir Horace Jones and the engineer was John Wolfe-Barry. It was opened in 1894. Initially the approach road only went as far as Tooley Street but in 1902 this was extended south. It took the line of Bermondsey New Road in its southern part but the construction of the northern part required the demolition of tannery buildings, one of the tenement blocks in Fair Street and the destruction of part of St Mary Magdalen's churchyard.

In the mid 1860s major changes in policy towards roads stimulated the demand for road transport. Firstly, tolls on the turnpike roads were abolished after 1866. Secondly the Metropolitan Board of Works (MBW) - this was a London-wide authority founded in 1855 and the London County Council's predecessor - recognised its duty to carry out improvements to an already overloaded network. In this area it did so most dramatically by the construction in 1864 of Southwark Street which linked Borough High Street with the Blackfriars Road. The MBW also carried out piecemeal but major widening to Tooley Street and was responsible for the demolition of Newington's most important building, the parish church of St Mary, when Newington Butts was widened in 1876. A replacement church was built on the east side of the road farther south while the abandoned church yard grimly hangs on as the Elephant & Castle's remaining open green space.

One great stimulus to this change in policy was the increased use of roads by private carriages and expanding public transport. Public horse drawn buses appeared from the 1830s and these omnibuses generated many new, short journeys taking much trade away from the hackney coaches and hansom cabs. Motorised buses appeared from the late-1890s.

In the 1870s another form of road transport came on the scene; horse trams. The building of lines, along Camberwell Road and the New and Old Kent Roads in 1871, Peckham Road and Queens Road the following year and along Great Dover Street and Newington Causeway in 1874, was every bit a fevered as the railway boom of the previous decade. As the railways had provided a better service and so displaced omnibuses over longer distances, so the trams did over short ones. Trams had a much greater capacity than omnibuses and operated at only slightly higher costs. They could therefore provide a cheaper, more frequent, reliable high-capacity service: average fares for example were only 2d and a typical service was that on Newington Butts, which ran at only four minute intervals. Soon after their introduction passenger numbers were, on average, three times those using horse buses.

Social conditions

The social conditions of much of Southwark, Bermondsey, Rotherhithe and Newington were a world away from those a short train ride to the south. These conditions were an inevitable consequence of accelerating industrialisation, the rise in population and its increasingly high density. Despite a generally bleak picture of social conditions they were not universal as there were areas of respectable working-class housing such as Bermondsey south of Jamaica Road and even of middle-class residences in Trinity Square, Newington or along the New Kent Road.

By the early years of Victoria's reign many of the grand, middle-class terraces, such as those on the Walworth Road and the squares to its west, had been subject to increasing sub-division, poor maintenance and the addition of new structures in previously spacious front gardens. Where there were undeveloped areas, such as the one provided by the closure of the Surrey Zoo site in 1878, they were filled by houses smaller and meaner than those already standing. The poorest areas were the Bermondsey and Rotherhithe riverside, and around Tabard Street and Mint Street in The Borough.

It had become apparent to those providing housing that the traditional two-up two-down terrace (initially intended for one, or possibly two small families but frequently occupied, by many more) was quite unsuited to the demands placed on it. Developers started to erect taller buildings: three-storied houses became common, such as those on Brook Drive, off Kennington Road, as did their logical extension, tenement buildings such as Devon Mansions, formerly Hanover Buildings, of 1875, in Fair Street, Horselydown. For the very poorest the common lodging house such as those in the Mint, the notorious area to the west of Borough High Street, provided the most meagre shelter.

A key to the quality of housing was less its location, but the landlord, or freeholder. Many landlords were

Below:
The Booth poverty survey map of 1889. The high concentration of black and blue colours confirm the poverty of much of the district.

Key
- ■ Lowest class, viscious, semi-criminal
- ■ Very poor, chronic want
- ■ Poor
- ■ Mixed
- ■ Fairly comfortable
- ■ Well-to-do
- ■ Wealthy

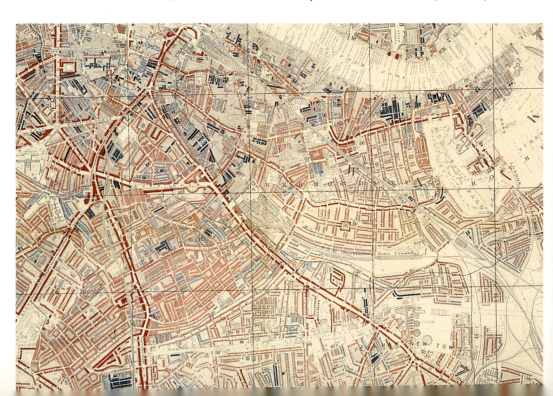

Right:
The Peabody Square
on Blackfriars Road.
A view of c.1872.

Industrial Classes was founded in 1841 and provided tenement buildings, such as Cromwell Buildings in Red Cross Way, built in 1864. Joseph Peabody, the American philanthropist, built only his second London development in Blackfriars Road in 1870. While today we would consider the style of all these buildings harsh and barrack-like, they were a major improvement compared to the conditions and facilities their tenants had previously endured. Large numbers of these so-called model dwellings were erected in the later years of the century. A particularly large scheme was the Guinness' Trust one at Snowsfields, Bermondsey, which housed 1700 people. These initiatives excluded the very poorest as, for example, rents on the Peabody estates had to be high enough to provide the required 5% return on the capital invested in their building. Tenants were also regulated by strict agreements, particularly regarding sub-letting and children.

Smaller in effect, but more generous in approach and spirit, was Octavia Hill. She managed all Church property south of the Thames and her idea was

overwhelmed by the numbers seeking housing and were unable effectively to enforce tenancy agreements even if they had wanted to. Many also observed that commercial use of land and property offered a far higher profit than housing. These factors, together with the absence of any minimum regulation or government enforcement, meant that many landlords allowed their properties to become slums.

The first large-scale, planned alternatives to the negligent private landlord did not come from the government, but from philanthropists. The Metropolitan Association for Improving the Dwellings of the

to replace unsuitable buildings with small-scale cottage-style homes in an attempt to generate feelings of ownership and responsibility in the tenants. The best-known example of this was in Red Cross Way (the cottages she built date from 1887), but there were others in Ayres Street and in Walworth. She was backed by ample capital and, as the church had not been the most conscientious of landlords, plenty of sites on which there was sub-standard housing. The only restriction to her programme was the amount of time she was able to elicit from supporters and this was crucial in preventing her from redeveloping as many sites as she had hoped to do. Like Peabody, she selected her tenants carefully and managed them firmly, requiring prompt and full payment of rent. She may have improved the housing conditions of only a very few, but with her policy of dealing personally with individual tenants she brought a new style to housing management and the problems of urban poverty.

Public bodies, locally the Vestries and London-wide the Metropolitan Board of Works and, after 1889, the London

Above:
The Earls Sluice. The sluice, which was alternatively known as the Black Ditch, was a notorious open sewer until the 1870s. It also formed the boundary between Rotherhithe and Deptford (and between Surrey and Kent). A watercolour of 1826 by George Yates.

Right:
Children in the Tabard Street area of The Borough, c.1890.

County Council (LCC), were given increasing powers over poor housing. Initially these were simply powers of inspection, later they were empowered to order the owners of slums to rebuild sub-standard premises. However, it was not until the 1890s that the LCC was given the authority for it to build new homes on any meaningful scale. There were frequent reports of overcrowding, such as in Tooley Street in 1856 when eight families, a total of 41 people, lived in eight rooms in the same house. Ordering the closure or demolition of such rookeries only intensified the problem as there was no obligation on the landlord to rehouse the tenants that had just been made homeless. More fundamentally, neither the Vestries, the Metropolitan Board of Works, the LCC, nor anybody else, could tackle the root cause of the overcrowding: the need for families to live close to places of work at a time when, for the poorest, work was casual but often only found after much searching.

After 1890 the LCC was empowered to provide housing and important housing schemes were carried out at Webber Row (near St George's

Circus) and, at Falcon Court (to the west of Borough High Street), and the first stage of much needed improvements in the Tabard Street area of Bermondsey was completed.

As well as appallingly overcrowded housing, the working-class areas of the Victorian city are also associated with other standards of public health scarcely imaginable to us. Southwark suffered outbreaks of all major diseases, experienced conflicts between reformers and the disinterested, was central to the reformers' activities and was touched by all aspects of their work.

If any one event made disease and public health a London-wide and national issue it was the outbreak of cholera in 1832. Cholera first appeared in London at Rotherhithe. This was a grimly appropriate location for its arrival given Rotherhithe's role as a place for the import of goods. There were significant numbers of deaths in the poorer parts of Bermondsey and Southwark, amounting to about 10% of the population. The cause and disappearance of the disease were as mysterious to observers as its violence. This outbreak prompted the first government enquiries into issues of health, and a tentative relationship between poverty and disease was established. Many of those involved in the investigation had been utterly unaware of the living conditions of the poor and were deeply shocked by the conditions they witnessed. One report of 1843 established that 30,000 of Southwark's residents had no access to piped water. No effective changes were forthcoming; legislation to deal with water supply excluded London and the Vestries, the City of London and later the

Metropolitan Board of Works were all opposed to central government intervening in local affairs.

During the 1840s the disposal of human waste became a problem because of the increase in the urban population and the more widespread use of the flushing toilet. Hitherto such waste had been disposed of in cesspools or carried away as night soil. In 1848 the Metropolitan Commissioners of Sewers were established. They undertook more thorough maintenance of existing sewers and required new properties to be connected to sewer system. Ironically, their practice of cleaning the sewers by flushing them went some way to making the second outbreak of cholera in 1848-9 more violent than it need have been. While people were beginning to grasp that there was a relationship between infected waste and disease, it was thought that the disease was air borne. While sewer-flushing cleared the air, it returned the source of the infection straight back into the River Thames, the area's water source. Meanwhile, in a outbreak of cholera, 1,535 Bermondsey and Rotherhithe residents died; 17% of the population.

A major breakthrough came in a study of 1849, based on evidence collected in Southwark by Dr John Snow, linking cholera with sewage-contaminated water-supply. Despite this the Southwark and Vauxhall Water Company, which served the area, was allowed to continue to take their supplies from the river until 1855. During this time, in 1854, cholera struck again, claiming another 16% of the population.

In the 1850s the upper Thames was developed as the source for drinking water and the reservoir at Nunhead, built to store it prior to consumption, dates from this period.

Dilute sewage passing as drinking water was not the only public health problem in early-Victorian inner-London as the burial of the dead was a growing public concern. Due to a rapid increase in the population the number of burials was exceeding the rate of decay of those already interred. Many churchyards were grossly overcrowded and burials were often made on recently disturbed plots and at wholly inadequate depths. This led to situations that were as undignified as they were unhealthy. Although the matter was raised in a government report of 1842, due to bitter opposition from undertakers and the parishes, no effective action was taken, until the closure of the existing burial grounds in the period after 1855. Each Vestry was empowered to open a new cemetery outside the metropolis, but not one of the urban Southwark parishes did. Rather, they left the deceased's family to find a burial place and many were interred in the huge Brookwood Cemetery near Woking where the costs of transporting the coffin, efficiently dealt with by the so-called necropolis railway operating from Waterloo, were more than compensated by the low cost of a grave-plot.

For the wealthier there was one cemetery close at hand. Nunhead Cemetery, to the east of the hamlet of Nunhead was opened in 1840 by the London Cemetery Company. It was a private venture. The company bought 130 acres of land and gave over 52 of these to the cemetery.

This picture of public health and housing reflects badly on the authorities of the day who appeared to ignore the problems around them. It is all too easy however to judge them by our own standards. During the 1840s and 1850s there was no proper understanding of the relationship between insanitary conditions and disease and few investigations had taken place into the living conditions of the urban poor. There were unprecedented levels of overcrowding and new factors, such as the water closet, put overwhelming demands on the existing, but primitive, provisions. Neither central government nor local administrations saw it as their duty or responsibility to intervene to improve the affairs of individuals, nor were there organisations or structures available to those that may have wished to instigate reform. Equally, there were no resources available to tackle the problem as, in an age before a real distribution of wealth, the greatest problems were in the poorest areas. When, latterly, central government did take initiatives, it was often faced with determined opposition, from the water companies who supplied (and poisoned) many of the area's residents, from the City of London, which on principle resisted attempts to have its long-established independence challenged, from landlords and from local officials and Vestrymen who, generally, did not see public health as an area that should concern them.

The main force of reform came in the end from central government through the work of Edwin Chadwick, who initiated many pioneering investigations and gave the duty to improve matters to reformed and new local authorities. In 1855 the Metropolitan Local Management Act transformed the ancient Vestries into 38 new units, and a new London-wide authority, the Metropolitan Board of Works, was established.

Government reorganisation

The new Vestries were largely based on the old parish areas, though two new units were created in the area: the St Saviour's Board of Works covering the St Saviour and Christ Church parishes and the St Olave's Board of Works covering St Olave, St Thomas and St John Horselydown. The new Vestries took on the functions of the old Vestries, plus responsibilities for street paving,

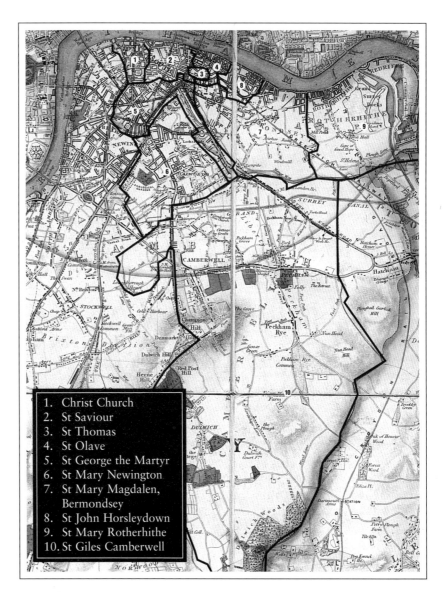

1. Christ Church
2. St Saviour
3. St Thomas
4. St Olave
5. St George the Martyr
6. St Mary Newington
7. St Mary Magdalen, Bermondsey
8. St John Horsleydown
9. St Mary Rotherhithe
10. St Giles Camberwell

lighting and watching (a primitive neighbourhood watch), which were transferred from the numerous Paving Commissioners. They were also given new powers and responsibilities for example for the construction of local sewers, the inspection of dwelling houses, slaughterhouses and other nuisances. Their responsibilities widened in scope as the century progressed to include for example, after 1875, the inspection of foodstuffs and after 1891 the collection of refuse.

More importantly they had to appoint and receive a report from a Medical Officer of Health. Frequently these reports drew stark attention to the conditions of the day and sometimes vigorously challenged the vested interests, which were seen as the main obstructions to reform. They reported vital statistics and causes of death. Infant mortality was particularly high and remained so until the end of the century: 40% of children died before their fifth birthday. In addition to cholera, tuberculosis, scarlet fever, typhus and influenza all claimed significant numbers of lives. These reports also

suggest the squalid conditions prevalent in the numerous common lodging houses as the death-rate among their residents was double that of the population as a whole. The Vestry also inspected offensive trades and the leather trade gave much cause for comment. One unlucky inspector reported that one of the Rotherhithe railway arches was being used for the storage and processing of large quantities of dog excrement, which was used in the leather tanning process. In the tanners' misguided vocabulary, this noxious substance was technically known as 'pure'.

The inspectors or Medical Officers of Health often advocated robust action but met with resistance to their proposals from the Vestry members. One such conflict took place in St George's parish where the Medical Officer of Health, Dr Rendle, resigned as a paid employee to become a vestryman when his pleas for improvements were obstructed. He acerbically observed of his colleagues in St George's Vestry that 'low rates rather than low mortality are made the test of public prosperity'.

Above
Bermondsey Town Hall of 1881 in Spa Road.

The Vestries also took on the provision of baths and washhouses. This was made possible by legislation dating from as early as 1846. The baths in Spa Road, Bermondsey opened in 1854 and were the first in south London. Manor Place baths were opened by the Newington Vestry in 1898. The Vestries were also responsible for opening public libraries. Bermondsey's library in Spa Road was opened in 1891, Newington's, in the Walworth Road, in 1893 and St George's, in Borough Road, in 1899. In the provision of these the Vestries were often assisted by the philanthropist Passmore Edwards. In the very last years of the century the Vestries became interested in new technologies and in 1899 both Newington and Bermondsey started to generate their own electricity for street lighting.

The Vestries were proud of their achievements and this pride was often translated into the provision of suitably grand office accommodation. Newington's Vestry Hall on the Walworth Road dates from 1865 and Bermondsey's from 1882. The most important member of the Vestry's staff was the Vestry Clerk, usually a solicitor by profession. If St George's Vestry is typical, he could expect to be paid less than the Medical Officer of Health, but considerably more than the treasurer (often the most important and best-paid person in modern local government). Other premises owned by the Vestries were depots such as Newington's in Manor Place. These were home to their vehicles and carts and also to large amounts of stabling for the numerous horses they owned.

The Metropolitan Board of Works' activities were in the areas of larger sewers and other schemes of London-wide importance. Its achievements were remarkable. Under the direction of its Chief Engineer, Joseph Bazalgette, it was responsible for the construction of London's main drainage system. Bermondsey was drained by a sewer that followed the line of the Lower Road and Evelyn Street; Walworth by the low-level sewer that followed Albany Road and the Old Kent Road; Camberwell and Peckham by the southern high-level sewer, and East Dulwich, Dulwich and Nunhead by the Effra branch sewer. These congregated at a pumping station in Deptford.

The Metropolitan Board of Works was also responsible for the creation of Southwark Park. Work on it started in 1864 and the park was finally opened in 1869. It occupied 63 acres of what had been market gardens. Although wholly in the parish of Rotherhithe, much to the frustration of local residents, it was called Southwark Park as it was in the parliamentary borough of Southwark

The other achievement of the Metropolitan Board of Works with

a local impact was the establishment of the Metropolitan Fire Brigade in 1865. Previous to this the fire service was provided by the London Fire Engine Establishment, essentially a co-operative formed in 1833 of the brigades' of the fire insurance companies. Its outdated equipment led to its conspicuous failure to deal with the Tooley Street fire which burned for two days in June 1861 and in which the Superintendent, James Braidwood, died. The London Fire Engine Establishment was disbanded and a new service with its headquarters in Southwark Bridge Road was established.

Further social reform came in 1867 when the arrangements for dealing with the poor were again changed by the Metropolitan Poor Act. This Act built on the principle of 1834 by creating new, and larger, Poor Law Unions, replacing provision that had hitherto been made in smaller parish units. It also allowed for the establishment of district asylums for the sick and many of the area's hospitals, such as St Olave's on the Lower Road, Rotherhithe, and Dulwich Hospital on East Dulwich

Grove have their origins in this act. The Act also allowed for some redistribution of monies between local authorities. This was important as it was the first time there was a meaningful reallocation of resources from rich districts to poor ones.

The Boards of Guardians were not the only providers of welfare. Some parish churches made modest attempts to provide some social relief such as St Mary Magdalen, Bermondsey, which in the 1890s, ran a Christmas gift scheme and loan club. More conspicuous in the final years of the century was the establishment of missions and settlements. Most of these had links with nonconformist denominations. They aimed to provide education and assistance to the needy, to be a centre for social activity and to spread their version of the Gospel. One prominent example was the Bermondsey Settlement which was opened in 1891 by Wesleyan Members of the Universities of Oxford, Cambridge, Edinburgh and London. Its warden was the Methodist Minister John Scott Lidgett. It had its headquarters in Farncombe Street. Its activities included classes that attracted, for example, in 1895, over 1000 pupils, a debating society, a choir and orchestra, a working girls club, a boys brigade company, the provision of coals and food to the very poor, the visiting of the sick, and a district nurse. Its leaders also involved themselves in local administration taking on the management of schools or as members of the Poor Law Board.

Other examples were Time & Talents, which was established in 1898 and provided food and education to the Bermondsey factory girls (these were a large, intimidating and not necessarily grateful body of beneficiaries), the Browning Settlement in Newington, founded in 1895 and so called because the its parent church was where the young Robert Browning worshipped earlier in the century, and Charterhouse in Southwark, based near Tabard Street. Other, similar institutions, often providing medical help, had their origins among students at Oxford and Cambridge Colleges, the Oxford & Bermondsey Club founded in Abbey Street in 1897 being a notable example.

One organisation that had a dramatic impact on both the landscape and the lives of the young was the London School Board, which was established in 1870. It was widely acknowledged there was a massive under-provision and initial estimates, later found to be too low, indicated that more than 11,000 children in Southwark, Bermondsey and Rotherhithe alone had no school to attend. The Board undertook a vigorous building programme and by 1883 it was operating 38 schools in these areas. The ancient grammar schools, originally founded by the parishes St Saviour and St Olave, moved twice in this period; firstly in 1855 to mock Tudor buildings to the north of Tooley Street, and then to a larger classical building nearby in 1895. The schools were amalgamated in 1899.

In 1889 the London County Council was created. For the first time London became a county and the new Council inherited the functions, assets and liabilities of both the Metropolitan Board of Works and the ancient County Quarter Sessions. The communities of Southwark, Newington, Bermondsey, Rotherhithe, Camberwell, Peckham and Dulwich passed from the county of Surrey into London.

Church, entertainment and commerce

It should not be thought that north Southwark was entirely a landscape that provided fodder for Charles Dickens' lurid descriptions, or shock to the socially conscious or compilers and readers of Commons' Select Committees; nor was it a world in which most peoples' lives were affected by official institutions; in fact government still worked with a light hand. Rather the social fabric of the area was woven by bodies a step away from official control: the church and in the later part of the century, retailers and the providers of leisure and recreation.

It is commonly believed that the Victorian period was a particularly religious one and the level of church building by all denominations would suggest this to be so. To cope with the increase in population the Anglican Church created thirty five new parishes. A number of these new churches, such as St Augustine, Lynton Road, were built by Henry Jarvis. The Church of England also rebuilt St Saviour's church, which had fallen into considerable disrepair, and at one time

was threatened with demolition. The retrochoir (the area behind the high altar) was restored by George Gwilt and the nave was rebuilt between 1890 and 1897 by A W Blomfield.

The Anglicans did not have a monopoly on church building. The Roman Catholic Cathedral of St George, designed by A W Pugin, was built between 1841 and 1848. Other Catholic churches in the area were the Church of the Most Precious Blood in O'Meara Street, dating from 1892 and Most Holy Trinity Dockhead built between 1834 and 1838.

One of the most striking church buildings in the area - its impact is heightened by its drab surroundings - is the Metropolitan, or Spurgeon's, Tabernacle at the Elephant & Castle. This was built from 1859-61 for the popular preacher Charles Haddon Spurgeon and was designed to seat 6,000 people. Some of his Sunday afternoon congregations were reported to exceed 10,000.

Despite this provision, Victorian Southwark, Bermondsey and Rotherhithe were not particularly

Godly places. The census of church attendance taken in 1886 showed that only around 25% of the area's population attended church. Parishes such as St Mary, Bermondsey regretfully observed in 1896 that large portions of their parishioners were hostile to the church.

Often disapproved of by the churches were places of popular leisure; pubs and music halls. Southwark and Bermondsey had no shortage of either. In 1900 Southwark and Newington had around 350 licensed premises and Bermondsey and Rotherhithe 270. There was one pub for about each 500 people. Many of these were of some antiquity such as the Angel in Rotherhithe but the later years of the century saw the demolition of many of the ancient Borough High Street Inns such as the Talbot and the White Hart. Prominent new pub buildings included the Thomas à Beckett in the Old Kent Road, which dates from 1898, or the Elephant & Castle, which was also rebuilt in ostentatious style in the same year.

For all of their vigorous campaigns against the demon drink, the churches

St. George's R. C. Cathedral, Southwark

were largely ineffective in curbing the level of consumption among the working classes. Undoubtedly heavy drinking caused great unnecessary hardship to many families but it was also the only way many could escape their circumstances. Women were almost as likely to be drunk as men; at the turn of the century they accounted for 40% of those arrested for drunkenness and 33% of those arrested for being drunk and disorderly.

Many pubs incorporated other entertainments. Common was the provision of musical entertainment and the music hall had its origins in the public house. Southwark, and especially the area near the Elephant & Castle, was particularly noted for its music halls. The South London Palace of Varieties was one of London's first purpose-built music

halls. It could seat 4,000 people, so rivalling the nearby Spurgeon's Tabernacle; each attracting an audience that was largely mutually-dismissive of the other. The South London Palace attracted the most popular performers of the day such as Marie Lloyd and Dan Leno. It is appropriate that one of the greatest entertainers of the early twentieth century, Charlie Chaplin, was born in Walworth into a music hall family. The area was also quick to welcome the arrival of the moving picture, and from the late 1890s cinemas opened in converted buildings.

Street sellers when advertising their wares also provided entertainment of sorts and these street sellers, or costermongers, have long been a feature of local street life. Walworth Road had a particularly busy market, but due to increasing road traffic and

the coming of the trams, it was increasingly forced into side streets. All sorts of goods could be purchased, from fruit and vegetables to fabrics or pets. The tradition of pearlies, a couple chosen from among the costermongers who arranged for charity collections, dates from the 1880s. The main shopping streets were the Walworth Road, Borough High Street, London Road, the Old and New Kent Roads, Southwark Park Road, Tower Bridge Road and Jamaica Road. Department stores, selling a wide range of clothing and household goods were, in spirit, not far from modern shopping centres. Prominent were Isaac Walton & Co. in Newington Causeway and Carter's, a men's outfitters, on the Old Kent Road. There were also many small general shops, open long hours, as the lack of refrigerators ensured a constant need for fresh food.

Above left
St George's Roman Catholic Cathedral. The building was designed by A W Pugin; a much higher tower was planned but never built. The building as shown existed from 1848-1941 when it was extensively damaged by enemy bombing. A postcard of c.1910.

Above right:
The Tabard Inn on Borough High Street. An engraving of 1875, shortly before its demolition.

CHAPTER 8

The Twentieth Century

To abuse a cliché, the twentieth century has been a century of two halves. The first fifty years were ones of vigorous social reform, relative prosperity and self-confidence; the second fifty were years of post-war rebuilding, depopulation and industrial closure. The modern townscape of northern Southwark is almost unrecognisable when compared to what existed before World War II.

The turn of the century was a clear watershed in the area's history: Queen Victoria's death was overshadowed in importance by the formation of new units of local government, the Metropolitan Boroughs, by the peak in population, which thereafter declined steadily and, after 1914, by a new, vigorous intervention in the lives of ordinary people by government.

In some senses writing about the history of the present century is harder than writing about earlier ones. This is not because there are fewer primary sources to use on which to base one's account; there are many more. Rather, it is because there are relatively few solid

secondary sources available: many classic texts of antiquarian local history were written at the end of the last century, many of the more general, but academic, works on the area or region have simply ignored the modern period, seeing twentieth-century Southwark as less interesting than the preceding centuries or than its surrounding areas.

There are many primary sources available, especially for the earlier part of the century: many local newspapers were published, (and cut and indexed by library services); businesses produced in-house magazines such as Peak, Frean & Co.'s *Biscuit Box;* the Metropolitan Boroughs and the London County Council produced printed (and indexed) minutes to their meetings, annual reports and statistical information about themselves; photography reached its maturity, indeed the Edwardian period was the zenith of postcard production - assisted by four local postal deliveries daily, the postcard was used as the means of rapid local communication in the days before the telephone - and map-making also became more common with organisations annotating maps for their own purposes.

In comparison with outer London areas the Southwark area changed relatively little between 1900 and the start of World War II. For its residents however the changes were huge. The population of the area dropped considerably. It peaked in 1901 with figures of 206,000 in Southwark, 131,000 in Bermondsey and 260,000 in Camberwell. This total, of 597,000, was nearly three times the figure of today. Southwark had the highest population density of any Metropolitan Borough. There was a huge rise in the general standard of living. This was achieved through the provision of health services and municipal housing schemes. Ordinary people started to become involved in local affairs as, through the extension of the vote and the emergence of the Labour Party, many felt that they now had a hand in controlling their destiny. This new sense of self-confidence and civic pride was further compounded by the creating of a separate Anglican Diocese of Southwark in 1905 and the redesignation of St Saviour's parish church as a cathedral.

World War I

World War I is most commonly thought of as taking place in Flanders' trenches, impinging only marginally on the lives of those left behind. While the most important and moving accounts of the war all come from the fields of battle, the war touched the lives of those left behind more than is commonly realised. Bermondsey, Camberwell and Southwark all made important contributions of men and services to the war effort and also suffered loss of life and damage from one of the war's lesser known aspects, Zeppelin raids.

Working class areas were prime grounds for the recruiting sergeant. Many young men had feelings of patriotism and bravado in almost equal measure, making them easy prey. The recruiter's job was further eased as many young men wished to escape the great hardship that characterised much of their lives: few could have imagined how much more awful the trenches would be than anything they had previously experienced.

There were three local regiments, broadly following the administrative boundaries. The 21st London Regiment was based at Flodden Road, in Camberwell. It was also known as the 1st Surrey Rifles. The 22nd London Regiment was based at the drill hall in Abbey Street and represented the Bermondsey area, while the 24th London Regiment, based in Braganza Street, Walworth, covered Southwark. At the outbreak of war these regiments started recruiting vigorously and were assisted by the local councils, who

gave over part of their town halls as the enlistment office. In addition Camberwell Town Hall was the main recruiting station for South London and a staggering 100,000 men were enlisted there alone.

Local communities, businesses and institutions also made a great contribution to the war effort. Numerous buildings were put to use as temporary hospitals, such as the building that was to become the Maudsley Hospital. Local firms responded to orders from the War Office, for example Peek, Frean & Co. made biscuits and other foodstuffs, Hallet, in Bermondsey, made antimony (used in the manufacture of shells) and Hobson made military uniforms.

During the war many women were engaged in traditional men's work while men were in combat. This work gave these women money, skills and power. Other women also had responsibility thrust on them through the widowhood that trench slaughter brought. This new status was reinforced in 1918 when women were awarded the vote.

Left:
Air-raid damage in Keetons Road, Bermondsey in 1915.

Above:
The Dockers' call-on shelter in Redriff Road in 1923. Most dock work was casual and it was from here that foremen chose their workers from the crowd of waiting men.

Above right:
An aerial view of the London Bridge area in 1921. Note both the level of activity on the river and the number of pedestrians on London Bridge.

South London also experienced for the first time a terrifying element of modern warfare: air raids. Whereas the number of air raids launched on London was nothing like that of the World War II, there were almost no precautions to protect the civilian populations. The relatively small number of deaths in the area was quite out of proportion to the damage to morale that the raids brought.

Southwark's industries remained buoyant during the first part of the century. The docks expanded. In 1904 the Greenland Dock was enlarged and a new lock was built to accommodate the increasingly large ships. A Royal Commission, appointed in 1902, resulted in the formation, in 1909, of the Port of London Authority. This

was a trust made up of the bodies that had an interest in the port. However, it still retained casual labour as the basis for hiring its workers. The Surrey Docks was the centre for the import of grain and timber. Much of the timber came from Scandinavian countries and the various Norse churches and missions, some of which were established in the previous century, were very active in this period. The Port of London Authority had no powers over the wharf companies and the largest of these, the Hay's Wharf Company on Tooley Street, was the chief place of import for dairy goods from the Empire. At this time London was importing more than 50% of the nation's butter and 70% of its cheese and most of this was being handled by Hay's Wharf. The company expanded

in the 1920s and in 1928 they built themselves a new headquarters, St Olaf House, so called because it was built on the site of ancient church of St Olave, which had stood just to the south-east of London Bridge.

1919-1939
Between the wars the amount of new factory building in Southwark and Bermondsey was relatively small but Camberwell and Peckham broadened their industrial base. Notable additions were the gummed paper manufacturers, Samuel Jones, who expanded their premises in Peckham Grove in the 1920s. Patriotically, so to speak, they adopted the Camberwell Beauty butterfly as the emblem for their products. Another addition was the Roberts Capsule and Stopper

Company, whose fine premises on the north side of Peckham Rye were built in 1932.

Southwark and Bermondsey, as centres of traditional manufacturing, were hit by the depression of the 1930s rather harder than most other areas of London. Bermondsey's unemployment rate reached 19% in 1932, compared to a London average of 12%, and as late as 1938 Southwark's rate, at 11%, was 4% above the London average.

Residents had increased opportunities to spend money or enjoy their spare time. In the field of commerce, many of the shopping streets reached their maturity and the street markets in East Street and Westmoreland Road came under Council control, ending the unsatisfactory situation (from the traders' point of view) of unregulated pitches. For many, real holidays also became a possibility. For those who could not afford a trip to the seaside, a month on a Kentish farm picking hops provided an alternative. Hopping was more a change of scene than a holiday. Hours were long, the work was hard and accommodation spartan, nor were the temporary workers always welcomed by suspicious residents.

Metropolitan Boroughs; housing and health

In the field of government, 1900 saw the establishment of the Metropolitan Borough Councils. There were 29 in London and three, Bermondsey, Camberwell and Southwark were established in this area. Bermondsey was made up from the Vestries of Bermondsey, Rotherhithe and the St Olave's Board of Works, Camberwell from the area of the Camberwell Vestry (in acreage it was the fourth biggest in London), and Southwark from the Vestries of St Mary, Newington, St George the Martyr and the St Saviour's Board of Works. These bodies inherited the functions, powers, assets and liabilities of the Vestries and were given many new functions as the century progressed. In addition their establishment removed the City of London's administrative powers over the town of Southwark. Much of the history of the early part of the century is related to the activities of the Boroughs and the London County Council.

The most dramatic change in the townscape of the area was in housing. The period before 1914 had seen only a small number of municipal housing schemes but the inter-war period saw a huge increase. In 1914 the majority of houses in north Camberwell, outer-Bermondsey and Rotherhithe were in Victorian terraces, and in Southwark and inner-Bermondsey there was a mixture of terraces and larger model dwelling schemes. This had changed significantly by 1939. Most of the initiative came from the LCC. By 1936 it had provided 4,800 dwellings in the area of the present Borough. They were unevenly distributed: 1,000 were in Bermondsey, over 2,200 were in Camberwell and 1,600 in Southwark. The apparent imbalance of these figures can only be explained by reference to the housing policies of the respective Boroughs.

The Metropolitan Borough of Camberwell built only 442 dwellings. As a consequence of Camberwell's relative inactivity, the LCC operated a vigorous housing policy in the area. The East Dulwich Estate, on Dog Kennel Hill was erected from 1933-6. It provided nearly 900 homes and was

Opposite:
Plans of the area covered by the Wilson Grove Estate before and after demolition. The homes built in the 1920 are, by present standards, not particularly large. The two plans shown are of the same scale revealing just how small the demolished houses were. Note in particular the back-to-back houses in the court just north of Janeway Street.

Opposite right:
The LCC's East Dulwich Estate on Dog Kennel Hill in 1936.

HOUSING SCHEME · BOROUGH OF BERMONDSEY
·PLAN OF SITE · SALISBURY STREET · AREA·
·AS EXISTING·

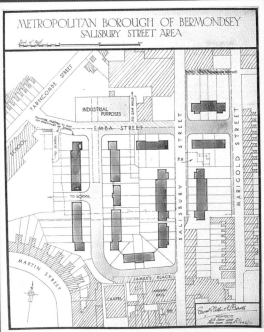

METROPOLITAN BOROUGH OF BERMONDSEY
SALISBURY STREET AREA

SOUTHWARK: AN ILLUSTRATED HISTORY

the second largest estate built by the LCC within London. As the estate was built on previously undeveloped land, was unusually large and was occupied by people who moved from slum accommodation, it was, in spirit, akin to the LCC's larger cottage estates outside London, such as Downham or St Helier.

Southwark also provided some housing for its ratepayers, but the figure, compared to the LCC's provision, was modest. By 1938 it had provided over 360 homes. The City of London, which through the Bridge House Estate still owned large areas of Southwark and Camberwell also provided municipal housing.

Bermondsey provided a startling contrast. During the 1920s and 1930s, the Borough had a policy of vigorous slum clearance and replacement by local authority-administered housing. It estimated that 75% of its dwellings were below standard and aspired to provide suitable accommodation for all those inadequately housed. It was also hostile to the idea of rehousing people outside the area. The Council also had its sights set on better

accommodation than the tenement-type blocks being built in many parts of London. It wished to build cottage-type estates similar to those being built on undeveloped sites outside London. Given that this aim was utterly unrealistic - there was simply not enough room in Bermondsey to provide housing of this sort, and the LCC and central government were opposed to the idea - it is testament to the determination of the Council that in 1924, the area around Salisbury Grove, which contained one of London's few examples of back-to-back housing, was knocked down and the Wilson Grove Estate erected in its place. It is a unique example of a municipally built, cottage-style inner London estate. Subsequently the Council was forced to become more realistic and all other new homes,

71

such as the Neckinger Estate, were of the tenement type. By 1938 it had erected 2,252 dwellings and actually owned 3,350, making it the largest municipal landlord in London. Despite this intervention, private landlords and a very small number of owner occupiers controlled more than 75% of properties.

The expansion of Council-run rented housing was a major change in direction but for many it was not in line with their aspirations. People wished to move away from the inner area and the population of inner-Bermondsey and Southwark fell steadily from the 1920s onwards. Of the people who did move, those of modest means moved to the LCC's cottage estates outside London (the LCC administered more dwellings

outside London than in it). Many wished for more than just the chance to live away from the inner-city; they wanted to own their own home. Many people, and particularly those in skilled or clerical jobs, were able to move to developing suburbs like Bexleyheath taking advantage of new, affordable housing, jobs on the growing Thames-side industries or quicker, more reliable travel to London on new roads or electrified trains.

While the people leaving were looking for the open spaces of the suburb, one of the Boroughs, Bermondsey, was doing all it could to bring the bring something of the countryside to the city through the work of its Beautification Committee. There were two main elements in this plan. The first was a programme of tree planting on pavements. By 1927 the Council had planted over 6,000 trees, mainly poplars and planes. The second was the development of horticulture by the acquisition and laying-out of open spaces. As well as shrubs and plants the council also provided playgrounds for local children. In the playground converted from St James' churchyard was the so-

called Joy slide provided by Peek, Frean & Co. No site was too small for their attention and even the most modest of spaces in front of Council buildings were adorned by plants or window boxes. Residents were also encouraged to participate through flower shows and window-box competitions.

The provision of playgrounds shows the Council's approach to be as much practical as decorative and also highlights one of its main priority groups, children. Children were central in public health, an area of work in which Bermondsey had a high reputation throughout London. Residents should have been grateful that the Council made this a priority, because it was certainly an area of great need. In 1904 its infant mortality rate (i.e. the number of deaths of those aged under one year expressed per 1000 births) was 172. The London-wide average was 139. Bermondsey's rate was exceeded only by Shoreditch and Southwark.

The Metropolitan Boroughs provided a whole range of health-care facilities (except hospitals). This work was under the supervision of the Medical

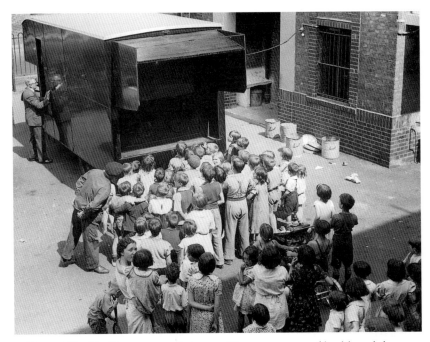

Officer of Health. He oversaw clinics, monitored social conditions, sanitation, and the health aspects of housing, provided health services (such as child welfare, dentistry, the care of diseases) and inspected food and drugs.

Bermondsey has gained its reputation for health care mainly through the work of its Health Propaganda Department. The Council had its own film unit under the supervision of the Medical Officer of Health, Dr Connan.

Films on aspects of health and the work of the Council generally were shown on a van that toured the area. There were also programmes of lectures, poster campaigns and pamphlets. In this ground-breaking work, which inevitably attracted much public attention, the Council was in advance of any other in the country.

It provided facilities other Councils did not. For tuberculosis sufferers it provided a solarium - it was thought than sunlight helped prevent the onset of the disease in those predisposed to it. When the solarium opened in 1926 it was the first of its kind in the country. Unique to London, Bermondsey mothers had access to the Council's own maternity and convalescent home, Fairby Grange in Kent, where a two-week stay cost as little as 10 s. (50 p). This service was used by about 16% of all mothers.

Despite these provisions, Bermondsey's reputation was not entirely deserved. Its residents were not significantly healthier than those elsewhere, in 1938 the infant mortality figures were 60 for Bermondsey, 59 for Southwark, and 66 London-wide: Southwark's fall was greater than Bermondsey's. Bermondsey and Southwark also had, for the period before the war, comparable levels of notifiable diseases. In tuberculosis care Camberwell ran more clinics than Bermondsey or Southwark, and Southwark children were more likely to be seen by a doctor than those in Bermondsey.

Hospital care was provided by the Poor Law infirmaries, which gradually evolved into general

hospitals. In 1930 the Poor Law Boards of Guardians were wound up, the workhouses were closed and the hospitals transferred to the London County Council. The busiest of these hospitals was St Olave's, which served the Bermondsey area. In 1938 it dealt with over 8,000 out-patients. The other LCC hospitals were St Giles' in Camberwell, and Dulwich, which was previously the infirmary to the Southwark area. There were also specialist hospitals in the area, such as the Royal Eye Hospital, the Maudsley Hospital for those with mental illness, and the Evelina Children's Hospital on Southwark Bridge Road. Guy's Hospital, as an old foundation, supported by land it owned and a government grant, was independent

of the LCC. While its number of beds, at under 700, was about the size of a general hospital, it was far more active in its out-patient services. In 1938 it had the third most active out-patient department in London. Health-care was also provided on a voluntary basis by the many missions, such as the Bermondsey Medical Mission, established in 1904 and numerous dispensaries.

Not all health care was municipal. Though on a smaller scale, the work done by the Pioneer Health Centre, more commonly known as the Peckham Experiment was equally ground-breaking. This was a private institution established initially in a house off Queens Road in 1926, but in 1935 it moved to purpose built premises in St Mary's Road. It was established by Dr Innes Pearce and Dr Scott Williamson, who were carrying out an experiment - they called it their laboratory -to see how access to community-based health and welfare facilities providing for all aspects of the preventative health of an ordinary (as opposed to a particularly deprived) population could contribute to the quality of life.

Left:
The Metropolitan Borough of Southwark's Health Services Department in Walworth Road in 1937.

Local families from the immediate vicinity were invited to become members of the health centre. They contributed a small subscription. Members were given a family health overhaul (but not treatment, it was a health centre, not a sickness centre) and had access to the centre's facilities. These included a swimming pool, a cafe, a general recreation area and dancing. The centre became a key focus for the social life of the area it served. As with Bermondsey, there was considerable emphasis given to the health needs of children.

Even today the Bermondsey Borough Council is spoken of approvingly, in part this is because there is a sizeable body of long-standing residents still in the area who benefited from the Council's work. The Council had strong ethos of municipal care. This was largely due two of the most influential people ever to have been active in the area's political life, Dr Alfred Salter and his wife Ada. The Salters dominated the local scene for most of the inter-war years. Alfred Salter came to Bermondsey as a medical student at Guy's; moved by the poverty and need of the area he

established a medical practice on Jamaica Road. Because of its high standard of care, accessibility and low charges, the practice gathered a huge following. The Salters, by then married, realised that their social mission could not be fulfilled by this work alone and so Alfred entered politics. He was a founder member, in 1908, of the Bermondsey Independent Labour Party. In 1922 the Labour Party, took control of the Bermondsey Borough Council and Ada Salter became its mayor, the first woman mayor in London. The Council embarked on their programme of vigorous social reform. In 1922 Alfred Salter was elected as Member of Parliament for West Bermondsey and for the next 23 years, until his death in 1945, worked unstintingly for the area.

Some of the Salters' views did not sit comfortably with a vigorous, male-dominated working-class community. The Salters were both Quakers and their religious beliefs informed their political ones. As pacifists both abhorred violence of any sort. During both World Wars they supported the cause of conscientious objectors and

Below:
Alfred Salter. Salter deliberately travelled by pedal bike in order to avoid alienating himself from residents.

unwisely persuaded the local Labour Party to oppose the implementation of municipal civil defence measures in the years before 1939. He was puritanical in his moral beliefs, hostile to monarchy (indeed any sort of unjustified privilege) and, in an area that had one of the biggest concentration of pubs in London, he vigorously espoused the teetotallers' cause. His overriding quality was one of energy this, combined with his strong views, did not always make life comfortable for colleagues and allies, who were required to see his plans to fruition and whose achievements were eclipsed by the Salters courting the limelight. Despite their uncompromising views they were held in very high respect by many people. His work as a doctor, their relentless championing of Bermondsey's cause, his equally vigorous support of the workers' cause, their local home, their personal generosity (Fairby Grange, the Borough's maternity convalescent home was theirs) and support of smaller ventures such as a co-operative bakery and a bookshop ensured their continued high esteem in the local mind.

In education, the London School Board was wound up in 1904 and its responsibilities were transferred to the London County Council. In 1900 it maintained 83 elementary schools (i.e. for those between ages 5 and 14) in the area (23 in Bermondsey, 35 in Camberwell and 25 in Southwark). By 1905 the LCC was providing more than 80% of London's school places. In 1938 the average roll in one of the elementary schools was 700. Secondary education was largely provided by older endowed schools such as Wilson's Grammar School in Camberwell or St Olave's & St Saviour's in Bermondsey, which were only part funded by the LCC. The LCC only fully funded two schools: Bermondsey County and Honor Oak. Dulwich College remained entirely private.

The LCC also had a hand in the provision of further and higher education. They maintained the Camberwell College of Art in Camberwell Road. This was founded in 1893 when the philanthropist, Passmore Edwards, provided money for the building of an addition to the Gallery. In 1938 it was the second

largest College of Art in London. he LCC also funded the London College of Printing, which moved to Stamford Street in 1922, and another much smaller technical college, the Leathersellers', in Drummond Road in Bermondsey. The Leathersellers' Institute was under the control of the biggest further education establishment in south London, the Borough Polytechnic Institute. The polytechnic provided technical and trade related education through evening classes and industrial and domestic education for boys and girls through day classes. In 1938 it was the second largest polytechnic in London.

While the needs of the young were being taken care of, the needs of the old were not neglected either. In the very early years of the century, the Liberal government introduced many pieces of social legislation, among them an Act establishing state-run old aged pensions. The Browning Settlement in Walworth played an important role in its adoption as the Settlement's Warden, the Rev. Francis Herbert Stead, was the secretary to the National Pensions Committee.

Opposite:
Laying electric tramlines in Walworth Road in 1904. The number of people and the size of the queue of trams show how important a contribution the trams made to London's transport.

The first half of the century saw improvements in transport methods rather than infrastructure. In road transport the tram reigned supreme; in 1913, for example, they made more daily journeys than buses (18,500 as opposed to 16,700) and a busy spot, such as London Road near the Elephant & Castle, could see nearly 3,000 journeys daily. Tram services, now under control of the LCC, were greatly improved by electrification in 1904. The horse was not entirely redundant as it continued as the main form of traction for buses and private road vehicles until the 1920s. After that date the petrol and diesel engine achieved prominence. At this time there was a short-lived experiment with steam driven buses, and the garage used until 1919 by the National Steam Car Company still stands on Nunhead Lane. Public transport received a great boost with the creation of London Transport in 1933. Its formation formalised existing co-operative agreements between potentially rival bus companies.

A new underground railway the Bakerloo, with a new station at Elephant & Castle, came to south London in 1906. The City and South London Railway was amalgamated into the newly christened Northern Line in 1937. With the exception of the London Chatham & Dover line from London Bridge to Victoria via Peckham Rye, which was electrified in 1909, overground rail services were slow to adopt electric power. The rest of the system was not electrified until 1925-8. Nunhead and South Bermondsey stations were rebuilt at this time.

There was one important addition to the roads' network, the construction of a new river crossing, the Rotherhithe Tunnel. Originally the LCC planned a ferry crossing but this was opposed and powers were given to build a new tunnel in 1900. Work started in 1904 and was completed in 1907. Compared to the nearby Thames Tunnel, its construction was swift and painless.

World War II

While the fires of the 17th century and the railway building of the 19th century both caused major disruption, undoubtedly the most traumatic period in Southwark's history was the years of World War II. Situated between the airfields of Kent and the centre of London, and containing prime targets, such as docks and railways, Southwark inevitably suffered destruction on an unparalleled scale. By the end of the war over 2,500 civilians had been killed and virtually every house damaged. Industrial targets suffered terrible bombardment, the Surrey Docks for example being all but destroyed.

The Metropolitan Boroughs were responsible for the provision of civil defence. Anderson shelters (makeshift tunnel constructions of timber and galvanised steel partly covered with earth) appeared in most gardens, but for those without a garden the Boroughs made other provisions. The Southwark and Bermondsey areas were handicapped in this respect as much of the land was low lying, soft and frequently wet, making the digging of deep shelters almost impossible. A poor alternative was inside railway arches; immediately underneath an obvious target. The only really secure shelter was deep underground and one such refuge was available, in a disused tunnel of the underground railway, which went to the City. The tunnel, known as 'The Deep' was over half a mile long and could accommodate 15,000 people. The Boroughs were also responsible for first-aid stations, the issue of gas-masks, decontamination stations (in case of gas attack) fire watching and air-raid warnings. In the event of raids they provided rescue services, temporary housing and storage for personal belongings. The London County Council were responsible, for hospitals, evacuation and, until 1941, for the fire service.

At the onset of the war, in September 1939, 35,000 children were evacuated, about 50% of the school population. The first months of the war saw almost no enemy action over London and by January 1940 most of the evacuees had returned to their families. The blitz, which started in September 1940, caused much destruction to life and property. From September 7th there were 55 consecutive days of bombing after which time it only gradually declined in frequency. Parachute mines, which exploded just above ground level, were particularly damaging. Unsurprisingly, two of the incidents with the biggest losses of life were at railway arches when they were being used as shelters. Seventy seven people died in an arch at Druid Street, Bermondsey, in October 1940 and 68 at Stainer Street the following February.

Bombing raids on the area were more intermittent in 1942 and 1943 until, in June 1944, a new weapon assaulted London, the V I. This was a pilotless flying bomb powered by a primitive jet aircraft engine. There were over 150 incidents involving these until, in September 1944, a new and altogether more deadly and powerful weapon appeared, the V II, a rocket-powered bomb. Less than 20 landed in the area but they were immensely destructive. The V II that landed at Waite Street, Camberwell in February 1945 killed 18 people and injured another 78. Both the V I and V II were random in their operation, although the V I caused more fear as it was never known when its engine would splutteringly die and the weapon fall to earth. The V II, was supersonic and gave no warning of its arrival.

To support the war effort the Boroughs organised collections of money and other goods. Given the overall level of poverty in the area and the massive disruption to people's lives, their generosity was astonishing. Bermondsey, for example, was responsible for raising nearly £8 million during the war period. Public parks, small as they were, were turned into market gardens and, in one of the most unusual pieces of support, Bermondsey's watercarts, normally used to water dusty, gravel-covered, summer streets, were taken to Normandy after the beachheads had been secured, to water equally dusty airfields.

Local manufacturing was hugely important particularly the Bermondsey food producers. There were also military projects that took place in the area. South Dock was used for constructing the Mulberry floating harbours and the Harland & Wolff yard also produced parts. On a different level, Glenlea, one of the large houses on Dulwich Common, was rented by the Dutch government-in-exile and used as a safe house for its secret agents.

The blitz spirit - honest co-operation between family, friends and neighbours in support of country and community - is mostly associated with the working-class communities of south-east and east London. It is no myth: there are numerous memories of shelter sing-songs, the sharing of rations, individuals working long hours in their jobs and then just as long as a volunteer for the civil defence. But just as the war brought out the best in people it also brought out the worst. Looting of damaged properties was not uncommon (though rarely reported) as was petty thieving from the docks or vandalism to air-raid shelters.

Below:
The Metropolitan Borough of Bermondsey goes to war.

1945 - today

Modern north Southwark is essentially a post-war landscape. It is open to debate as to whether this landscape is more due to the destruction caused by air-raids, or professional planners. Certainly the task of post-war reconstruction was viewed with relish. There was an unprecedented sense of self confidence, encouraged in industrial areas by the election of a Labour government and the prospect of greater state involvement in people's lives. The 1950s and 1960s saw a rebuilding of industry and housing.

Industry, though battered, did not desert the area and within only a short space of time factories were functioning, sometimes in improved premises. By 1951 the Surrey Docks were working to their pre-war levels and expanded beyond this level, reaching a peak two years later.

However the post-war industrial boom was not to last. Gradually manufacturing started to desert Southwark, Bermondsey and north Camberwell. Between 1971 and 1986 the Southwark area as a whole lost about half its manufacturing jobs. Traditional industries disappeared rapidly: by 1986 only one Bermondsey tannery remained; the food industry lost nearly 4,000 jobs and prominent closures were Peek, Frean & Co. in the mid 1980s and the Anchor and Horselydown breweries, which were closed in the 1980s. The Borough has not fully recovered from this decline and continues to endure high levels of unemployment. In 1992 unemployment was at 18% and male unemployment 25%. The young and those from ethnic minorities have been particularly badly hit in this respect.

Preceding and precipitating these closures was the closure of the Surrey Docks in 1970. The Surrey Canal closed at the same time. This was a huge blow to Rotherhithe and Bermondsey but not an unexpected one. The docks' gross tonnage had been falling since 1964. Goods were transported by progressively larger ships, which could no longer enter the Surrey Docks; goods were increasingly containerised, and timber, central to the Surrey Docks' activities, was being packaged in larger quantities inappropriate to the antiquated handling methods in the docks; road, not rail or canal, was the preferred transport method away from the docks and inner-London's congested streets were inappropriate for this. Suddenly in 1970 a huge area, which for over two centuries had been a hive of activity, was left eerily vacant.

The post-war need for housing was immense: in 1948 for example 8% of Bermondsey's housing stock was unfit for habitation, the highest figure in south London and squatting was widespread. In the period to 1955, 9,600 new homes were provided in the area of the present Borough comprising 11% of all new homes in London. These were provided in roughly equal numbers by the Boroughs and the LCC. A fair number of these homes were designed to be temporary, but prefabs became more enduring and popular than their builders could have imagined. However, the post-war period is most associated with the building of flats, both low and high rise, on an overwhelming scale.

The earliest municipal post-war flats were very similar in design to the pre-war tenement blocks. Brenley

House on Tennis Street in The Borough is an example. Soon new materials and building methods became available. This resulted in new slab-like blocks best shown in the Sceaux Gardens Estate (1955-9) behind Camberwell Town Hall on Peckham Road. This slab style was superseded in the 1960s and 1970 by high-rise blocks such as Castlemead on Camberwell Road, the twin blocks of Rotherhithe's Canada Estate or the LCC's Brandon Estate (1957-8 and further extended in the 1960s). The rate at which these blocks were built was artificially fuelled by government grants, and concerns about the quality of the building or the surrounding environment were secondary to the speed of construction. The Utopian tone of the brochures that accompanied the official openings was rapidly superseded by widespread unpopularity among the tenants.

Tower blocks never quite replaced the slab style of building and this made a revival in the late 1960s and 1970s. Most notable creations of this era were the Camden, North Peckham and Gloucester Grove Estates, which continuously connect the area between Peckham Road and St George's Way, and the Aylesbury Estate north of Albany Road. All were designed to segregate vehicles and pedestrians by using elevated walkways. This idea was taken to its most extreme on the Aylesbury Estate, the scale of which is quite vast (it provides 2,434 homes). Its many critics are joined by Nikoulas Pevsner, the writer on architecture, who commented that 'an exploration can be recommended only for those who enjoy being stunned by the impersonal megalomaniac creations of the mid 20th century'. The estate was designed by Southwark Council's architects department.

Modern building has also taken place elsewhere, such as the Bonamy and Silwood Estates in Rotherhithe and Dawson's Heights on Overhill Road in Dulwich. From a distance Dawson's Heights stands like a fortress guarding Southwark's southern approaches, but when nearby one realises the view from it is much better than the view towards it. In response to criticisms fashions in social housing have changed again and recent building, such as the homes built on the Bricklayers' Arms site, are a reinvention of 19th century brick terraces.

The population rose slightly after the war, but steadily declined after 1955. In 1961 it was 310,000; thirty years later it was down to 218,000. More dramatic than these changes have been the changes in the composition of the Borough's population. As early chapters have shown, Southwark has always given a home to immigrants (the Germans, Dutch and Flemings in the early modern period and the Irish in the 19th century) and the post-war years have seen the arrival of large communities, particularly from the Caribbean and Africa, and to a lesser extent ethnic Chinese, Cypriots, Vietnamese, Somali and Croatians. About one-third of the present population is from an ethnic minority and this figure will continue to rise as more than half the Borough's schoolage population is from an ethnic minority. There are 20 languages spoken in Southwark's schools, 6 of them by more than 1% of pupils. Southwark has a particularly large Black African population concentrated in the north Peckham area.

Above:
The Gloucester Grove estate. Walkways like these were a major feature of many housing developments of the 1970s and 1980s.

These communities, despite enduring considerable disadvantage in jobs and housing, have made a great contribution to modern Southwark. Dr Harold Moody, originally from Jamaica, was a prominent and much loved GP in Peckham Road in the pre-war period. Sam King, who arrived in 1948 on the Empire Windrush, the first ship to bring Caribbean immigrants to Britain, went on to be Southwark's first black mayor in 1983-4.

New communities unsurprisingly aroused negative feelings among resident populations and in the late 1960s the dockers, despite their exposure to goods from overseas, saw fit to support the overtly racist views of Enoch Powell.

It is appropriate that Southwark's newest residents are celebrated in Southwark's newest park as the multi-cultural gardens in Burgess Park contains plants from the new settlers' countries of origin. Burgess Park is unique as it it London's only park created from an area that once contained roads, houses, shops and factories. Its origin is in the 1943 County of London Plan, commonly known as the Abercrombie Plan, which identified north Camberwell as the part of south London most deficient in open space. The plan recommended the creation of a new park, to be situated between Albany road and St George's Way.

All levels of government, local, regional and national, underwent much change in the post-war period. The general direction was towards greater involvement in people's lives. With the creation of the National Health Service, responsibility for hospitals was taken from the LCC and public health from the Boroughs. However local politicians were able to retain a hand in their control through the creation of health authorities although this link was broken with the creation of health trusts. As populations fell so hospitals have closed. St Olave's on the Lower Road shut in 1984 and even Guy's has fought threats to it since the 1980s.

Education was reorganised in 1944 and many secondary schools were established for the 11-16 age group. At this time there were 73 primary schools and 45 secondary schools. The number of secondary schools fell dramatically as schools closed in response to a falling population, or merged into larger units or, have left the Borough in reaction to the policies of comprehensivisation. A prominent desertion was St Olave's & St Saviour's, which moved to Orpington in 1968 in order to retain its grammar status and expand.

A major reorganisation in regional and local government took place in 1965. The London County Council was abolished, and the Greater London Council (GLC), a new authority covering a much larger area, was formed. The LCC's educational functions were taken over by a new body, the Inner London Education Authority. At the local level, the Metropolitan Boroughs were abolished and larger, London Boroughs were created. The new London Borough of Southwark was formed from the three Metropolitan Boroughs and amid much protest from those with local allegiances. Bermondsey's residents were particularly aggrieved at losing their own Council.

Relations between the GLC and the Boroughs on one hand and central government on the other were especially strained in the 1980s. Central government squeezed expenditure, increasingly dictated the services to be provided and imposed policies, such as the right-to-buy (for those living in council housing) that were anathema to local politicians. In 1986 a left-wing and combative GLC was abolished. In some respects these actions captured the mood of the day as the Labour Party was losing support from its traditional sources as is seen most

clearly in the bitterly fought Bermondsey by-election of 1983, when the Labour Party lost control of a seat it had occupied continuously since 1924.

Another bitter blow to local and metropolitan politicians was being denied any control over the redevelopment of the docks. In 1981 the task of overseeing this work was given to an unelected body, the London Docklands Development Corporation (LDDC), a body, appointed by and responsible to central government. The London Borough of Southwark lost control of planning, economic development and highways in the whole of Rotherhithe and the Bermondsey riverfront all the way to London Bridge. The LDDC's methods and achievements are still open to debate. In its work it was given a head-start by Southwark Council, which by 1981 had drained the docks and laid out new roads.

The LDDC's aims were to provide homes, jobs and services. Certainly many new homes were created; in Bermondsey, particularly near Butler's Wharf, some conversions were of

quality and style but in Rotherhithe the flats are often a twee echo of the warehouses that once dominated the landscape and the houses are generally small. Many developments rely for their success on their proximity to the Thames or the remaining enclosed docks, the Greenland, South Dock, Surrey Water and Canada Water. The number of new jobs is considerably less than those lost when the docks closed. The only industrial establishment in sympathy with the previous manufacturing base is Associated Newspapers' (owners of the *Evening Standard* and *Daily Mail*) printing works, which opened in 1989. With regard to services, the most obvious new addition is the Surrey Quays shopping centre. It contains all the retailers to be found on the standard British high street.

Opposite page:
Recent developments near Surrey Docks.

Right:
The Coats of Arms of the Metropolitan Borough of Bermondsey, Camberwell, Southwark and bottom the London Borough of Southwark.

Top right:
Trader and customer at the stall area of the Elephant & Castle shopping centre.

Bottom far right:
Modern developments in Gainsford Street, Bermondsey. The Circle by CZWG of 1987-9. The sculpture of the drayhorse, Jacob, is by Shirley Place.

SHOPS AND OFFICES

AREA FOR NEW SHOPPING CENTRE

SPURGEON'S TABERNACLE

LONDON SCHOOL OF PRINTING

NEWINGTON BUTTS

LCC

ST. GEORGE'S ROAD

LONDON TRANSPORT ELECTRICITY SUB-STATION

LONDON ROAD

Of Southwark's other main shopping areas, only the Aylesham Centre in Rye Lane has been standardised in this way. The Elephant & Castle, Walworth Road, Camberwell Road, Southwark Park Road, Denmark Hill and Lordship Lane on the other hand still have a high proportion of non-chain shops. The very north of the borough is still devoid of a good shopping street, while the Elephant & Castle shopping centre desperately tries to draw attention to itself thorough is grotesque pink facade; a feature clearly visible from 5,000 feet in the air! Large supermarkets have

been a feature of recent years and, while popular, they have posed a threat to established, smaller traders. One enduring feature of Southwark's commercial life has been its street markets. The traditional markets on East Street and Westmoreland Road have been augmented since World War II by the Friday morning Bermondsey antiques market.

The redevelopment of the Elephant & Castle in 1958-65 was one of the biggest schemes undertaken by the LCC in south London. It had been a notorious bottleneck in the pre-war years and the subject of many

frequently deferred improvement schemes. Its extensive destruction during wartime gave sufficient impetus to start from scratch and the result, which scarcely considers the needs of those on foot, is another more overpowering bottleneck. On a similar scale were the the construction of the Bricklayers' Arms roundabout and flyover (at the junction of the Old and New Kent Roads) and the roundabout at the entrance to the Rotherhithe Tunnel. Despite these huge investments, today's smaller number of travellers move at peak times more slowly than their predecessors a century ago.

Above:
The redevelopment of the Elephant & Castle in 1962. The auspicious sunburst is symbolic of the planners' confidence in such schemes. Many today would view this portent with irony.

Postscript

Two characteristics stand out starkly from this survey of Southwark's history: relentless change and the overwhelming scale of Southwark's human experience.

Visitors today, who know nothing of Southwark's past, would see in much of the townscape of the north of the Borough modern commercial buildings with the occasional Victorian facade or school, or perhaps a very occasional 18th century terrace of houses. They would hardly be aware that they were in an historically distinguished part of London. Many of the sites they would be looking at have been occupied continuously for more than one thousand years and have undergone a score of rebuildings, additions and demolitions. On the other hand, Dulwich, only a short distance away, has been one of the most conservatively managed parts of London and sections of ancient woodland still remain.

The human scale of Southwark's experience is nowhere more overwhelming than in its population statistics: a century ago population densities in the northern riverside areas were six times that of today, infant mortality figures were five times those of today and its total population was nearly three times that of today. By contrast, at the same time, Dulwich had the second lowest population density in London. Other human statistics are equally striking: the 100,000 volunteers that enlisted during World War I at Camberwell Town Hall, or Sunday afternoon congregations of 10,000 in the 1860s to hear the preacher Charles Spurgeon. Other figures that record social achievement are also outstanding: the number of new homes built after World War II (9,600 in ten years), the number of classroom places provided by the London School Board (50,000 in the ten years after 1870) or the number of trams per day at a busy spot (3,000 at London Road in 1913).

Modern Southwark is still a place of great contrasts: along the riverside, as a result of the development of London Bridge City, is a thriving business district, home to financial institutions and national media. Not far south, in Newington and north Peckham, are large areas with characteristics all too typical of the post industrial inner-city: unemployment, bleak housing estates, cut-price shops - the human face of what makes Southwark London's second most deprived area. South again is the Victorian landscape of Peckham and Nunhead, and south again you find in Dulwich one of the wealthiest and most exclusive parts of London.

Southwark's past has not had the recognition it deserves. Too many writers pay only lip service to this area's contribution to the London conurbation. It is true that much of this contribution has been to provide a number of the elements no city has yet been without, but generally tends to ignore: industry, the poor (in overwhelming numbers), popular and bawdy entertainment, immigrants, criminals and prisons. As well as understating the importance of these factors, more positive achievements have also been ignored: advances in social welfare, the pioneering of new forms of transport, the survival and preservation of numerous fine buildings and the vitality arising from a social and ethnic mix unique in London. In fact Southwark's history is

Above:
The canopy above Peckham Town Square, focus for the area's redevelopment.

but did not become a diocese until 1905. Many important functions, such as the relief of the poor, or hospitals, or education have not always been in the hands of local administrations. However, a sense of community has grown this century and probably reached its most cohesive form during the traumatic years of World War II and those of optimistic reconstruction thereafter. Post-war industrial decline has been cruel to the area's self-confidence. However, people still strongly identify with their immediate locality - Bermondsey or even 'The Blue' (Blue Anchor), Peckham, the Elephant, Dulwich Village, or even Surrey Quays (this name is sadly but gradually replacing Surrey Docks)

so rich, that in a general survey such as this, one is forced to treat superficially some districts that, were they in another London Borough, would earn a much fuller account.

Southwark has also struggled to achieve a sense of identity. It has been important enough to return MPs since 1295, but not powerful enough in the medieval period to achieve full Borough status, nor in later years to repel the administrative control of the City of London. It was one of the largest settlements south of the river

One criticism that can be levelled at many developers involved in shaping the recent townscape is that they have been too quick to ignore the best of the past. This is a criticism that applies less today than it has done: new housing recalls Victorian brick terraces; the popular late-night entertainments of the Old Kent Road pubs and the club the

Ministry of Sound are in the spirit of the music halls, and the gastronomic delights of Butler's Wharf recall London's larder that was Tooley Street. The opening of the Thames Path means the river is again becoming a feature of many people's lives; a new Bridge (from St Paul's to Bankside) and a new railway (the Jubilee Line Extension from the West End to Greenwich via Blackfriars, the Borough and Bermondsey) will tie the area more closely to the centre, and the flagship development of the new Globe Theatre and the transformation of Bankside Power station by the Tate Gallery put Southwark firmly back at the centre of London's cultural life.

Southwark can look forward to the next two thousand years of its history confident that its past will be increasingly appreciated and that it fully earns the accolade of London's most historic borough.

Left:
Bermondsey Station on the Jubilee Line.

Left bottom:
The ticket hall at London Bridge Jubilee Line Station. This is the same location as the archaeological dig on p.3.

Below:
The new Globe Theatre on Bankside.

Illustrated pocket histories of the communities within the London Borough of Southwark

Beasley, John *The story of Peckham*. LB. Southwark, 1983.
Boast, Mary *The story of Bermondsey*. L.B. Southwark, 1984.
Boast, Mary *The story of 'The Borough'*. L.B Southwark, 1997.
Boast, Mary *The story of Bankside*. L.B. Southwark, 1985.
Boast, Mary *The story of Dulwich*. L.B. Southwark, 1990.
Boast, Mary *The story of Walworth*. L.B. Southwark, 1993.
Boast Mary *The Story of Camberwell*. L.B. Southwark, 1996.
Humphrey, Stephen *The Story of Rotherhithe*. L.B. Southwark, 1997.

Prettejohns, Graham; Mann, Brenda & Ilott, *Larry Charles Dickens and Southwark*. L.B. Southwark, 1994.

Boast, Mary *The Mayflower and Pilgrim Story Chapters from Rotherhithe and Southwark*. L.B. Southwark, 1995.

Davis, Rib & Schweitzer, Pam *Southwark at War*. L.B. Southwark, 1996.

V. Leff and C.H Blunden, *Riverside Story The Story of Bermondsey and its People*. 1965)

G.W. Phillips, *The History and Antiquities of the Parish of Bermondsey*. 1841

Brockway, Fenner *Bermondsey Story. The life of Alfred Salter*. Allan & Unwin, 1949 reprinted Stephen Humphrey, 1995.

Tames, Richard *Camberwell & Dulwich Past*. Historical Publications, 1997

W H Blanch *The Parish of Camberwell*. Allen, 1875, reprinted Camberwell Society, 1976

H J Dyos - *Victorian Suburb; a study of the growth of Camberwell*. Leicester University Press, 1961

Green, Brian *Around Dulwich*. Village Books, 1989

Green, Brian *Dulwich Village* Village Books, 1989

Survey of London *Vol XXV St George's Fields*. LCC, 1955

Survey of *Vol London XXII* Bankside. LCC. 1950

Beck *A history of the parish of St Mary Rotherhithe*. Cambridge UP, 1907

Book of Walworth Browning Hall Adult School, 1925

London Encyclopaedia Ed Ben Weinreb and Christopher Hibbert. Macmillan, 1987

Shepperd, Francis *London 1808-187 The infernal Wen*. Secker & Warburg, 1971

Pevsner, Nikolaus & Cherry, Bridget *London South* Buildings of England, Penguin 1983.

Rendle, W *Old Southwark and its people*. 1878

Carlin, Martha *Medieval Southwark*. Hambledon Press, 1996

Boulton, Jeremy *Neighbourhood and society: A London suburb in the seventeenth century*. Cambridge University Press, 1987

Conan, D M A *history of the public health department in Bermondsey*. Metropolitan Borough of Bermondsey, 1935

Johnson, David J *Southwark and the City*. Corporation of London, 1969

Golden Grace *Old Bankside*. Williams & Norgate, 1951

Walford, Edward, *Old and New London* Vol. VI The Southern Suburbs